Willian

For children

Penelope Farmer

William and Mary

cover illustration by Peter Richardson
text illustrations by Nancy Petley-Jones

Piccolo Pan Books

for Judith Davis
and for Clare and Thomas
who read it first

The four lines on page 115 are taken from 'At Dunwich' by Anthony Thwaite. The poem appears in his book *The Stones of Emptiness* (Oxford University Press, 1967).

First published in Great Britain 1974 by Chatto & Windus Ltd
This edition published 1977 by Pan Books Ltd,
Cavaye Place, London SW10 9PG

ISBN 0 330 25100 7
Printed in Great Britain by
Richard Clay (The Chaucer Press) Ltd, Bungay, Suffolk

chapter one

Lying there on her bed with the window behind her, she would still, she thought, have known she lived beside the sea. Not just because of the sounds the gulls made, but because she could see them reflected in the glass of her picture. Her bedroom had once been a bathroom. It was very tall and narrow like a tunnel and there still were yellow bathroom tiles halfway up the wall so that pictures had to be hung rather high above them. This one of dressed-up rabbits, left over from when she was small, she knew too well to notice much – and now, high as it was, she

could not see the rabbits at all – the glass reflected white to her. Instead the gulls with slow wingbeats fell in and out of it or else glided there, wings still, outstretched. Sometimes they almost hypnotized her into feeling she moved, she flew herself, as in a standing train when another moves slowly past.

She often lay like that in the holidays, doing nothing except watch the gulls and listen to pop music on her radio; and almost as often someone would come in and ask – wearily – if she had nothing better to do than that and how could she listen to that awful noise? The someone today was her mother, carrying heaps of papers and looking, as usual, neat but harassed.

'Turn that radio down, Mary. I can't hear myself think,' she added, which was normal, too, but she had put out a hand and turned it off before Mary had had time to move. Then she said, 'Hunter, you know – William – should be arriving soon. The car's gone to meet him. You've missed it now, but you could watch out for it coming back.'

'Should I? Must I?' Mary asked.

'It would be welcoming – and you don't seem to have anything else to do.'

'Why should I have to *do* anything?' asked Mary, who was always asking it, because most people here, she thought, did far too much; indeed they never stopped. Her headmaster father worked in his study both holiday and term alike; her mother was not only the headmistress of the school but also housekeeper and assistant matron, besides in term teaching creative English to the senior boys.

'Well, William should give you some good ideas for things to do. He's always full of projects in my classes.'

'Even so, he won't want me,' said Mary with conviction. She had used to look forward to it, when boys with nowhere else to go spent part of their holidays at school. But not any more – she was resigned to their taking very little notice of her. She did not blame them. Why should they want to play with her, a girl, and often, as it happened, younger, while there were dayboys living nearby that they could visit instead? Much more tiresome was her mother's attitude, eyeing her and whatever boy it was so benevolently – as if we were going to get *married* or something, thought Mary disgustedly; while what actually happened was that after any meal, whichever boy it was would ask perfunctorily, 'Do you want to come, Mary?' adding hastily, 'You'd probably be *awfully* bored,' and disappear firmly on his own, though he would tend to be quite nice to her in-betweenwhiles. In the holidays boys never teased her or accused her of telling tales to her parents as they did, collectively, in termtime.

William, she imagined, would be like all the others, or worse maybe. He had a reputation for being lone – for not appearing to care much about anything or anyone; so she went, still reluctantly, out of her room; out of her parents' quarters, small, safe and carpeted, into the long, uncarpeted school corridors, as soon as she pushed aside the curtains that divided home from school, setting up the small echo that seemed to follow her always in the holidays, making her feel like a small nut in the wrong, large shell.

She wandered in and out of empty, hollow-sounding classrooms, wrote her name on the blackboard in one, in three different colours; drew a face on the blackboard in another, in the only chalk available, which was blue; counted how many times a boy called Dunn Ma had carved his name on the desks in the same classroom (she counted twenty, seemingly impossible, but every desk had it once, and some two or three times). In the next classroom, flanking the front door, she went and stood by the window, waiting for William to arrive, drumming her fingers on the windowsill.

The bottom of the window opened at a slant, the top of the radiator reflected in it like a row of little teeth. She imagined herself in the mouth behind the teeth, imagined William walking in through the teeth into the open mouth; until the car drew up at the steps below the front door, and William's emergence, lugging a suitcase, startled her, because the imaginary William had made her forget the real one.

'It's very heavy,' he explained to Mary once he had noticed her, for she stood diffidently in a dark corner of the hall, so that he would not have to notice her unless he wanted to. 'It's got my books in it.'

'Hullo,' Mary said.

'Oh, hullo. That's the wrong way round,' he added, 'I should have said it first.' And explained, Mary looking blank, 'Hullo, I meant. Hang on a bit.' He left the suitcase and Mary for a minute in a stripe of cold air from the open front door; came back saying, 'Well, it's still there.'

'What is?' Mary asked.

'The sea,' said William. 'Joke,' he said, Mary looking blank again, as indeed she felt. 'Or sort of. I forgot to look before. Where am I sleeping?'

'In the sickwing – the cell. You always do in the holidays.'

Halfway up the stairs he looked back down at her and said, in an astonished voice, 'Aren't you coming?' For Mary still stood hesitant in the hall below. So then she ran up after him, followed him up the stairs, all the way along the passage. But when they turned down the little narrower passage into the sickwing, she waited again, outside the door of the room known as the cell, while William pushed a chair aside, threw his suitcase on to the bed.

It was like a cell exactly, a little single room the same size and shape as her own, but with a window much higher up and nothing in it, apart from William's trunk awaiting him, but a bed, the chair, and a washstand, a mirror above that, and a picture – of another chair – hung rather high on the wall in a frame too big for it.

She wished suddenly, very powerfully, that William could sleep downstairs with them in their flat; partly to keep her company, partly because it seemed so lonely for him up in this bare room. There was a spare bedroom next door to Mary's, but when she had asked once why the holiday boys could not use it, her mother had replied in a surprised voice, 'Oh, but that's for visitors.'

'But they *are* visitors,' Mary said.

'Grown-up visitors, not boys, of course.' Her mother's tone implied that Mary was being silly.

'But we don't have grown-up visitors,' she said, adding, 'or *practically* never,' diplomatically, at the look on her mother's face, for they did not. And had someone turned up unexpectedly (and she had never known them to), it would be easy enough for whichever boy it was to move upstairs. In the flat at least, it was less like an empty school. Perhaps boys did not feel so lonely as girls – but she thought they must. Some little boys cried wretchedly at night when they first came to school; she had heard them.

'Aren't you coming in, Mary?' asked William suddenly.

'You hadn't asked me.'

'Oh, for goodness' sake,' he said, but mildly. 'Come in and shut the door. It might be less freezing then.'

But in that bare room with nothing and no one to confront save William himself, she stared at the ceiling, tugged at her shirt, shifted from one foot to the other, did not know what to say or do, save look at herself in the mirror, which had an interesting flaw in it, a wave across the glass, so that, reflected, one side of her face looked higher than the other.

She wondered if she ought to help William unpack. But he did not look as if he needed help; laying things out so carefully, in such neat little piles, which he then set neatly into drawers; as tidy as Mary was untidy in spite of her mother's attempts to train her. Once, looking up, he seemed surprised to see her still standing there watching him, cleared a space, said, 'Why don't you sit *down*,' which Mary thankfully did. It was not fair, she thought, that he should be good at something girls were supposed to do well, whereas she was not; especially unfair because she was so hopeless at boys' things like Latin and football. None of the girls she knew had to do either of these things as she had to, being at a boys' school.

William had almost finished with his trunk by now. He turned to his suitcase, mostly full of books, as he had said. At the bottom, however, there lay unexpectedly, a vest, which he pulled out a little carelessly – something that had been wrapped in it fell out on to the bed. Mary turned without particular curiosity to see what this was, but William made a grab, picked it up again, and put it in his pocket, with a glance at Mary to see if she had noticed. So she pretended she had not and did not ask, only a little curious anyway to know what it might have been. She, too, had things she kept private to herself, though to anyone else they would have seemed unimportant. So she gazed steadfastly elsewhere until William said,

'Right, that's finished. What shall we do now?'

Mary looked helpless. 'What would you like to?'

'What do you do, usually, by yourself?'

'I sort of – well, I wander about,' she said reluctantly, because it seemed so feeble. 'You know – I go and draw on the blackboards in the classrooms, and I read a lot. I can play in the gym. And sometimes I go and paint in the art room.'

'You are lucky having them all to yourself. Isn't it nice?'

'I suppose it is,' she said with surprise, because actually it was, though lonely, and she was used to that.

'Do you go out?'

'Of course. Sometimes.'

'Well, let's go out. We can, I imagine. There aren't rules, like in termtime?'

'But where shall we go?'

'Down to the sea front? On to the beach?'

'But it's icy today. It'll be *freezing*.'

'Well, we can wear lots of coats, can't we?'

'I suppose we can,' said Mary, who did not expect such heartiness of William somehow. They went down the main staircase, forbidden in termtime. Midway, on a half-landing, there was a picture that had hung there as long as Mary could remember. If she shut her eyes, she knew its every detail. But still she could scarcely have told its subject, because she was so familiar with it. It was too dark there to see easily anyhow.

But William stopped and began to look at it. So now Mary looked too and made herself take it in.

It showed the destruction of a town by the sea, like theirs, but having no resemblance to it otherwise. For one thing, it was not imaginable that the people of her town should ever group themselves half-naked in such curious attitudes, twisting or sprawling and raising their hands to the sky. For another, they had here no neat and conical volcano belching out shapely flames, large sweeping ones balanced by little licking ones, reflecting red light upon the whole town, while pouring streams of lava down its slopes towards it.

The town in the picture consisted largely of pillared

buildings, mostly slightly contorted, as if the ground heaved up beneath them. And pillars were tumbling this way and that, but neatly and symmetrically, not at all higgledy-piggledy, as you would expect. People rushed about in the open squares between the buildings, they, like their writhing fellows, dressed in wide long robes that left fair amounts of them naked, and their arms too were lifted to the sky. If you looked very closely, you could see that they were shouting.

'Oh woe, I expect,' said William in Mary's ear.

'Oh *woe*?' asked Mary. She could not imagine what he meant.

'Those people, yelling, oh woe, like people in the Bible. I expect they are gnashing their teeth as well.'

On the right hand side of the picture was the sea. An enormous wave blossomed on its horizon like a flower. And the sea in the foreground was already creeping over the quays and beaches in curls and waves as neat and beautiful as the flames of the volcano behind.

A little rubbed gold plaque stood on the frame beneath the picture. William peered at it. 'Atlantis,' he read aloud. 'The Fall of Atlantis.'

'I *know*,' said Mary. 'Remember, I live here,' but as she spoke remembered that she had in fact forgotten, totally, and felt herself blush because of it.

They stood side by side in silence, still. Mary, peering into the picture, deeper and deeper, was almost beginning to feel that nothing else existed. It was as if she was exploring it, building by building, person by person, each and every sign of destruction too, the flames and waves and toppling pillars; but above all the sea, that great wave flowering upon the horizon.

She felt, did not see, William's hand move to his pocket and clutch at something. They were standing so close that whatever it was brushed the back of her hand. And then, for no reason that she was aware of, she found herself shutting her eyes. It was extraordinary, like shutting her eyes in a fast car. Dizziness took over the movement, and there was no stillness anywhere by which she could attempt to anchor herself, as she might have clutched at upholstery or a handle in a car. The movement began to involve herself as well. Her head became a twisting spiral, her body another larger one, each hand, each foot made a little one besides. Then she opened her eyes and for a moment did not know where she was. There were still people and falling pillars and buildings glowing red. Yet she and they had changed. The buildings had grown enormous, so had the people, or rather they were ordinary people-size, the same size as herself, because she was in the picture with them now. The picture had come alive all round her.

chapter two

For a moment, overcome by total panic, she shut her eyes again. But when she opened them, nothing had changed. Only she saw William standing next to her. He was not, apparently, alarmed at all, surveying everything in as calm and detached a way as he had surveyed the picture earlier.

'We'll be killed, William!' she said wildly. 'We'll be burned or crushed . . . we'll . . .'

William took her arm. 'No, we won't,' he said. 'Just watch . . .'

So Mary just watched, obediently. Everything con-

tinued as before. But in a little while she began to discover a pattern, a very odd but reassuring one. In spite of the flames, she saw, even though they escaped by hairbreadths no one ever actually got burned or crushed by the falling pillars (indeed, it could almost have been the same pillars falling all the time, though she never caught one righting itself and beginning to fall again). Flames licked close enough to warm her and William too, and they sometimes felt the wind of a pillar's fall. Yet they seemed to be in no real danger whatsoever. She gradually grew used to it, ceased to be so frightened anyway, became aware of other things, how cold her feet were, for instance (it was so cold in the hall, she thought, in the holidays; only they were not in the hall any more, or were they?) and how noisy it was with the roar of flames, the crash of falling stone, the wailing cries of people. The cries, too, developed a pattern of their own, and gradually she realized why: that just as William had suggested, everyone was shouting the same thing more or less in unison. 'Oh, *woe*,' they said, 'Oh *woe*,' and she began to giggle, because not only did they look so ridiculous, with their strange clothes and stranger attitudes, they also sounded ridiculous, as if they were all trying unanimously to subdue an invisible or else non-existent horse.

There was another sound too, lesser but very steady. Mary was about to ask in William's ear what this could be when a man stepped out of the throng quite close to them and inquired politely, 'Can I help you, strangers? Is there anything you might wish to know?'

He had a gold collar round his neck and wore a tunic that covered one shoulder only, leaving the other bare. His arms and legs were muscled, brown and strong, his hair black as a gipsy's.

'That kind of hissing, grinding noise ...' asked Mary. 'Can you tell us what it is?'

'You mean gnashing – of teeth . . .' The man, smiling, waved at the people fleeing all round them. 'They go together, you know – weeping, wailing, gnashing of teeth – to indicate distress . . .'

'Well, you don't look particularly distressed,' William pointed out, and indeed this man did not; with his muscles, such obvious healthiness, with his smile, white teeth in a brown face; with such whiteness and brownness altogether, he hardly looked real at all, he looked like a picture on a vase in some museum, or else like someone on a holiday poster for Spain or Italy or Margate even.

'Come to sunny Atlantis,' William said. 'Well, I told you they'd be gnashing their teeth, didn't I, Mary? Can you show us how to do it?' he asked the man, who at once opened his mouth very widely, showing more teeth than ever. Very slowly he brought the two halves of his jaw together, clacked them up and down, closed them tightly, and began jiggling the bottom of his face – at least that is what it looked like. Mary wanted to laugh and so, she could see, did William. But if you listened hard you could hear, very faintly, a grinding sound.

'Now,' said the man very encouragingly, 'now, you should try—' which William did, and a moment later, hesitantly, Mary too. She clacked successfully but ground less well till she discovered that what looked like jiggling was actually a way of moving your jaws round rhythmically, rubbing upper and lower teeth together. It made a loud and echoing noise inside her head, but from William and their teacher together came just little, slipping threads of sound, only audible perhaps because joined to the rest of it, all about.

Mary was concentrating hard. Next time she looked up the gipsy-looking man had gone. William took her arm again. He put his mouth to her ear and shouted right into it.

'I think we should join in everything.'

'Why?' Mary was shouting back, and, 'How?' But the noise had suddenly grown so huge again her shouts vanished into air. 'Rush about and wave your arms and shout, "Oh woe," and gnash your teeth,' William was instructing her ear by now.

'We've got the wrong clothes on,' protested Mary. But it did not seem to worry William anyway, for he was already running away from her, doing it all himself. So she too began slowly and reluctantly to move. She was very embarrassed at first and awkward; scarcely raised her arms above shoulder level, her 'oh woe-ings' whispers rather than shouts, while her feet moved only slowly in a a stumbling way, zigzagging her about, even so bumping her into people who pushed her aside rather crossly and went on again. But gradually it became easier. She began to feel a shape and pattern in the thing – not just in her own movements but in the ebbing and flowing of the crowds, so that she moved with them rather than against them, fitting her to-ings and fro-ings to theirs without any further collisions or even near misses, only the gentlest of brushings-past.

Sometimes she stood and wailed within a group, swaying and waving her arms. Sometimes she ran and darted about, arms outstretched, yelling her distress. It reminded her of drama classes she used to go to, and suddenly she found she was enjoying herself hugely, so ran and waved and shouted more furiously than ever (though she did not often remember to gnash) fearing neither the pillars nor the flames nor even the way the earth had begun to tremble and split in places now, for it still never happened where she was.

So she forgot to keep an eye on William. He was easy to see at first, his jeans and grey pullover plainly distinguishable amid all the flowing and pallid draperies. She soon ceased to worry, even to think particularly of watching him. And when her eyes next searched, she found she could not see him anywhere.

Terror returned at once. It came only from herself, for nothing had changed about her, only William was not there. But she panicked utterly, running in, about, and all around in search of him, through this crazily rocking and roaring world. Until at last she had no breath left to run and flung herself, gasping, on the steps of a pillared building, still somehow intact.

She was alone altogether now. In her fear she had run out of the central square into a maze of once stately streets. There were cries in the distance and growlings and rumblings. But here it was relatively still and quiet. She called for William once or twice. If he was anywhere close at all, he ought to have been able to hear her voice. But his name lingered and came back to her in a misshapen echo that faded almost at once into the muddle of more distant sounds. She began to cry, yet was scarcely aware of the tears falling on her cheeks, putting up a hand to brush them away, not knowing she was doing it.

She got up and started to walk on, picking her way carefully between the splits in the tremoring earth, her back to the glowing volcano, her face towards what she did not know. Even if she found William, she was wondering, however were they going to get home again? However had they got here in the first place? When she saw an open space ahead of her, between a row of buildings, she quickened her pace in order to still the thoughts, dodging and hopping and at last running again, until she burst out into it.

She found herself on the quays, on the very edge of the sea. To her far right where the bay curved round, she could see ships moored against other quays and tossing wildly. Here, though, was nothing but the sea itself, glowing red from the volcanic fires. And there were waves tossing, not ships, haphazard whitecapped waves, some big, some little, but all at cross-purposes, running into and over and round each other; mighty heaves meeting little pushes and both disintegrating into a mess of thin white foam.

The disorder made her feel dizzy to look at it. But it did not matter. For in the distance was the biggest wave of all, and now she could see that if all the other waves had been put together, they could scarcely have equalled it. So far, it had remained on the horizon, forever about to sweep in, yet forever poised, as in the picture in the hall. But now, as if she had summoned it, it began to move, rode in on the sea like a huge, dark monster with foaming jaws – higher than a house, then higher than a castle, then higher than a mountain, it grew and grew and grew.

Mary was transfixed. She stood watching it and could not move; watched it come on, nearer and nearer, and only when it was so close that spray from it touched her cheeks did she turn at last and start to flee towards the tumbling town, her movement as unreasoning as her standing still. She could never escape it now, no one could, for this was no pretending, harmless wave, as the other waves had been harmless, and the flames and earthquakes. With the ground heaving before her, she caught her foot and fell, half-raised herself, stretched out an arm, thought, fleetingly, that now she must look like one of the people in the picture writhing so beautifully, even if, compared to them, she was so wrongly dressed. Then, 'William,' she screamed, '*William* ...' For he was running towards her, dodging flames and waves and splits in the earth, holding something out – and as he reached her, as the pillars of the remaining buildings toppled behind him, the great wave rolled over them and broke upon the town.

But Mary opened her eyes to stillness and to darkness; the darkness of the picture only, with underneath the dim gold plaque. She looked at William, and William looked back at her, no expression on his face at all. And they continued downstairs as if they had never halted, as if what had happened had passed between footfalls merely.

chapter three

Mary woke up next morning feeling happy but for no special reason. She turned on the electric fire, climbed back into bed, and lay listening to the radio and watching the reflected seagulls till she judged the room was warm enough; what her mother would have called an unhealthy fug. Then she got up and mooched about, washing hardly at all and dressing very slowly, trying on a skirt before settling for a pair of jeans. She was not allowed to wear jeans or shorts in termtime because her mother said that even if she did go to a boys' school she must preserve her femininity. It was, Mary thought, very unfair, since in most matters she was expected to be like – that is, as good as – any boy, and since being a girl was what made this difficult, the more conspicuously girl-like she was the harder everything became, or so it seemed to her. Even so she did not bother much with jeans in the holidays, there being no argument. It was only because of William that she put them on today.

All this took a long time because every time the radio played a record she liked, she stopped to dance to it. So she had no shoes or socks on still when William walked in on her. He did not knock. She might, she thought indignantly, have been stark naked. But she did not suppose he would have minded, even supposing he had noticed it. Any more than he would have cared if she wore a skirt or jeans.

'Do you like that sort of music?' he asked.

'Some of it,' she said hastily, turning it off – her parents had told her so often that the noise was horrible, she had begun to think she must be peculiar to like it. Defiantly, she said, at once, 'Yes, I do; *all* of it. Why? Don't you?' The boys in termtime were not allowed transistors.

'Oh, some; hard rock,' he said, and snorted. 'Whatever that might be.'

'How can you like it if you don't know what it is?'

'I do really. My mother likes it, that's why – that sort of music. And I like the name – like undentable mountains.'

'To hear *my* mother – and my father – you'd think that was all it ever sounded like. And your mother *likes* it? Goodness.' She turned the radio on again, but only very softly.

They both stood at the window now, drumming on the panes. First William, then Mary, rubbed a clear space on the misted glass to help them look out. It was grey there and bleak. They could see the naked backs of hotels beyond the uneven waste of sand and grass that lay between the main town and the front. Their backs were even more stained and untidy than their façades, crisscrossed by fire escapes and having odd, sometimes jutting windows with sloping roofs placed without regard for order or symmetry.

Beyond, the sea was grey too and faded into a grey sky. The gulls wheeled and dipped as their reflections did, their cries only faint through the closed glass; ghostly sounds, but everything seemed ghostly to Mary today.

William was licking the lower, still misted pane of glass. She saw his tongue's pink reflection first, in the clearing it had made, but when she looked sideways found both tongue and reflection, one seemingly sprung from the other. So she put out her tongue and began licking too; without a word being said, it became a competition to see which of them could clear most the faster. They did not lick very long because it was already breakfast-time. But even when they reached the breakfast table, Mary's tongue was still cold from licking cold glass. It was an odd sensation because her tongue, it occurred to her, was one part of her that remained relatively warm or cool, usually, even when the rest of her was too cold or hot.

They ate breakfast in the staff dining room during the holidays, waited on by those of the kitchen staff who had stayed to help clean and sort and order; though they used china belonging to Mary's family instead of the ordinary school china. Her parents sat at either end of the table, William on one side, Mary and Miss Pitt opposite. Miss Pitt was the school secretary, a very tall thin woman, with very long feet, known throughout the school as Penelope Pittstop. Between her place and Mary's was a collection of pill bottles, for Miss Pitt suffered grievously from indigestion; at the end of every meal there was a little pile of onion or carrot or cabbage – whatever disagreed with her – discarded on her plate. Despite which she ate enormously – Mary had never seen anyone eat so much. Quite often they all had to wait for her while she consumed a second helping or a third, very slowly, because of her digestion and because she tended to talk a great deal too, rather mournfully and mainly about her niece in Australia. It had come to Mary's notice recently, after a long time, that her parents found this as, or even more, irritating than she did. She had caught them exchanging glances from time to time, very discreet, but once she'd grown aware of them, unmistakable. And sometimes her father would make an excuse to leave the table while Miss Pitt was still eating or, if he had something particular to say, broke in on her talking to ask, very politely, 'Would you excuse me, Miss Pitt, but there's something I have to say to Mary,' or some similar excuse. But the one time Mary had tried this herself, she had been silenced immediately by both her parents, and afterwards her mother had lectured her at such length and with such vehemence – how kind Miss Pitt was (and she was kind) and how much consideration she deserved, having no family to go to (except 'my niece in Australia', and I wish she would, Mary muttered to herself) – that Mary grew puzzled eventually. She had not after all been so very rude; and she did not really hate Miss Pitt, could not in fact imagine the school without her. Miss Pitt had been there at least as long as they had, since before she herself had been born.

Miss Pitt seized always on the obvious joke. 'William and Mary,' she said halfway through breakfast. 'Just like the king and queen.'

'Yes, isn't it,' said William very seriously. Then, staring straight at Mary and quite expressionless, went straight into a rhyme – starting 'William and Mary' – that Mary knew ended with a very rude line indeed. She waited breathless, half apprehensive, half amused, to see if he would actually say it. He reached the last line but one, paused, stared at her more intently than ever, yet still without a flicker of a smile, began the last line, 'Then Will . . .' and stopped abruptly. Casually he said, 'I've forgotten the rest of it – do you remember, Mary?' at which she collapsed in furious giggles and was told off sharply by both parents at once.

During the subsequent silence, Miss Pitt asked if they had planned interesting things to do that day. William and Mary looked at one another. Both knew what they wanted – at least Mary imagined William was as enthusiastic as herself – yet neither had dared discuss it. Yesterday, afterwards, they had not spoken, but had gone about the rest of the day as if it was ordinary, or rather William had, Mary merely took her cue from him.

'Isn't either of you going to answer Miss Pitt?' Mary's mother inquired.

'I don't know. I hadn't thought,' Mary said. 'I don't know what William's going to do either.' For she still half feared he might want to go off by himself.

'There's a nice Walt Disney in the town this week. Would you like to see it on such a bleak and nasty day? I tell you what, I'll treat you both, shall I? Would you let me treat you, Mary?'

But they did not want to go to the cinema. Mary sat scarlet with dismay.

'Mary, say thank you to Miss Pitt. It's so kind of you, Miss Pitt, I'm sure they'd love to.'

Liar, thought Mary, LIAR, knowing her mother did not think much of films in general and Walt Disney in particular, a fact Miss Pitt ought to have known after all these years. (The quickly exchanged glance she caught between her parents meant, she was certain, that they felt the same.) She said, 'Thank you, Miss Pitt,' very fiercely, and seethed with frustration and with rage inside. William, echoing that, glanced at her also in a way that looked to be more amused than cross, which did not help to calm her either.

'You needn't get so worked up,' he said, when they were back in her room again. 'You do get into such states about everything. We've got the whole morning still. And I'm not quite sure what you proposed we should do with it anyway. Were you going to abandon me and do something on your own?'

Liar, she almost said again, but still did not. She was not yet that easy with him. And she did not want to be the first to mention what had happened. Suppose it had all been some illusion of her own, not shared by William? She did not really believe that, yet felt herself close tighter and tighter within herself, the more because she felt that William still laughed at her.

There was a cleaner working in the hall when they reached the landing a little later. They waited upstairs, leaning over the banisters, while the hum of the vacuum echoed round the wooden walls. 'It's like being in a walnut shell.' William stared up at the domed wooden roof. When silence returned, both cleaner and vacuum departed, they went downstairs to the half-landing.

Mary felt sick suddenly, out of apprehension, longing, fear, excitement. Perhaps there was fear above everything. Momentarily, she wondered if she really wanted anything to happen, almost, positively, hoped that it would not. She was much more frightened than she had been last time, she thought, but remembered that then she had expected nothing. They stood before the picture with their eyes fixed on it. Then, as William's hand went to his pocket, they both shut their eyes, Mary finding the whole picture still burning itself upon her empty lids. All was just as before, except that this time there came no dizzying sensations. Now if she did not open her eyes, it was only because she would not, not because she could not. Her apprehension had entirely gone. She just knew that she wanted it to happen. She was almost grinding her eyelids together, clenching first her hands and then gradually her whole body, in order to encourage it.

'Open your eyes, idiot, open your eyes.' She heard William's voice and for a moment felt a wild hope, so opened them slowly to find only the picture as before and William smiling at her.

chapter four

There was no relief, just desperate disappointment.

'We must try again,' she said wildly. 'It *must* happen.'

'It won't.'

'How do you know?'

'I feel it in my bones. My bones are brilliant at things like that.'

'Well, I shall try all the same.' And she shut her eyes again but to no avail. Afterwards she said nothing more but went miserably downstairs looking at her feet, took her coat from the hooks in the porch where she had left it

yesterday, and with William went outside, down the steps, and towards the series of small alleys that led downwards to the sea.

'You shouldn't mind so much. I told you,' William said at last.

'But I don't mind. And you shouldn't boast,' she added, needing to attack him somehow. 'Your brilliant bones! I ask you, honestly.'

'Oh yes? I'll say you don't mind.'

'Don't *you* mind?'

'I don't think I expected anything, not really.'

'You might have warned me.'

'You wouldn't have believed the brilliance of my bones, in that state of mind. Anyway, we hadn't talked about it, had we? I was almost beginning to think I'd dreamed it.'

'We didn't dream it,' said Mary with conviction.

'And you do mind things too much, you know. It's like all those fights you have with boys in termtime. Some of them are scared of you – really.'

'I'll fight you in a minute. Why do you have to go on and on about it?'

'I dare you to fight me,' said William, grinning and shaping a fist.

But Mary shook her head and said no more, walking a little faster only, her ringing footsteps reminding her how she had used to be frightened of these alleys, thinking them hollow underneath because of the way footsteps resounded there between the high stone walls.

She could not keep up the pace she had started. William moved straight ahead steadily, and she had to make little hops round him to keep up. After a while she fell back and then actually had to run to catch up with him, feeling the slight, unfamiliar pull of jeans against her knees.

'Why can't you walk straight?' he said at last, over his shoulder.

'You walk too fast. That's all it is.'

When they stepped out into the waste space behind the hotels, the wind hit them with still greater force. But that was not the whole of it, as they discovered when they came up upon the road, where their heads were above the level of the sea wall. They fought their way across it literally. Then walked along the pebbled beach under the gaze of the shabby hotels – all with letters missing from the names across their fronts, so that Hotel Esplanade, for instance, read H TE ES LANAD – having to fight even harder to prevent themselves being blown sideways against the sea wall. The drifts of pebbles shifted under their feet, tipping them unevenly to and fro, at times almost seeming to hold their feet like magnets, at other times rejecting them. So they slid and slipped and shuffled their way along the beach, across the wooden breakwaters to the old pier that walked out into the sea, and sat there sheltered between its long and rusty legs. Looking up, they could see chinks of light between the boards. The wind threw itself at the pier in noisy gusts; it groaned and creaked among battered wood and iron but touched them only a little here.

The wind and sea together had blown everything out of Mary's mind. She had to think hard to remember what had been disturbing her, and when she did, a heavy sense of loss came over her again. William, whistling under his breath, picking up pebbles, examining them idly, did not seem concerned at all. Tentatively, she said, 'How do you think it happened? Might it happen again?'

'How should I know?'

'Would you like it to?'

William reflected. 'It was peculiar. It was quite nice.'

'It was frightening,' said Mary. And she asked again, asking the air as much as William, 'How did it happen?' and 'Might it happen again?'

William said nothing. But after a moment – Mary had been gazing out to sea, through the legs of the pier at a steamer crawling along the horizon: it tossed a little, unimportantly from here, though it must have been pitching wildly in that wild grey sea – she became aware that he was fumbling in his pocket. When she looked at him, he was holding out his hand. And on it was a shell.

It was like a very large mussel shell, curved, scimitar-shaped; its inside, though, more like mother-of-pearl, was pinkish and shiny, with rainbow colours reflected softly here and there. And when she took it and turned it over, she discovered that the outside was brown, instead of dark blue like ordinary mussel shells, a very delicate yellowish-brown, graduated in visible rings, darker at the base, lighter – yellower – towards the top. Its edge was slightly uneven and very sharp. As she moved it about the colour altered; sometimes it looked as much green as brown or yellow.

'Where did you find it?'

'I didn't. My father sent it to me.'

'It's nice. Where did he send it from?'

William shifted abruptly on the stones. 'Shall we go to that film this afternoon, Mary?'

'I suppose we might as well. If she's paying for us. And there isn't anything more interesting to do.'

'Oh, do stop feeling sorry for yourself.'

'I'm *not*,' Mary began, and then all indignation faded in the realization that William must have shown her his shell for a reason; and only one reason was likely or possible.

'Is that what you were holding yesterday when ...?'

'Why do you think I was showing it to you, dumbhead?'

'So perhaps it had something to do with it ...'

'Perhaps it did,' William said.

'Oh, I hope it works again.'

'That's taking us back to where we started; if it was the shell, that is.'

'It must have been, surely?'

'One factor possibly, but not necessarily the sole cause of that effect. It needs testing, as a hypothesis, anyway.'

'I don't understand a word you're saying.'

'You're not supposed to; I'm being clever,' William said.

'In which case,' said Mary, blushing a little, 'I understand you perfectly.'

The beach was very bleak and bitter. They went home quite pleased at the prospect of the film, though neither would have admitted this. And both, as it happened, quite enjoyed themselves.

*

'It was extremely good, for such a stupid story,' said William, as they emerged chilly and blinking into air and light.

'It was a pity though ...' Mary began, then stopped abruptly. It had been a film mixing cartoon characters with live ones. There had been an underwater sequence – candy-pink and baby-blue fishes with enormous eyes (and in the case of the lady fishes lengthy eyelashes and frilly aprons besides) dancing together in a turquoise-coloured sea, watched by two live, human children. Mary had looked at William then, feeling rather than seeing him turn towards her in the darkness. But at that moment the reel of film had broken, and the screen, after a flash of scribbles, had shown for the moment only dusty, vivid, but empty light.

There were stills in the frames beside the cinema doors. They both paused to look and found the fishes again and the turquoise sea. And then Mary knew at once what was to come; she had neither doubts nor uncertainties. Nor did William, obviously. He looked at her briefly, and his hand went to his pocket and fished out the shell and held it out to her. And Mary touched it and shut her eyes. Her hand burned at the touch of the shell. Her head spun, her body, everything – again she panicked, yet almost enjoyably. When the movement stilled a little, she wrenched her eyes open to find herself dazzled, as by neon lights, the colours here so vivid and unreal: the swimming-pool-coloured sea, the pink and blue and green fish. Some blew bubbles in tasteful and even patterns, while others waltzed efficiently, boy-fish with girl-fish in the proper way (on closer inspection the boy-fishes not only lacked eyelashes but wore spotted bow ties), to music which, though watery and distorted, sounded much like the 'Blue Danube', changing after a little while to the 'Thunder and Lightning Polka', played by a brass band.

They were standing on the seabed in an enormous rocky cave. Beneath their feet the impossibly smooth and pearly sand was patterned all over like a mosaic floor, the outlines of fish and starfish and sea horses made out of pebbles mostly and seashells, set deep into the sand. The walls and roof were studded with little pink cushions that gave off light – pink light, in spite of the vivid turquoise water; when Mary looked closer, she saw that they were all sea anemones, some closed, some waving little pink tentacles. And along the walls huge conch shells had been set upright in the sand and filled, quite dazzlingly, with seaweed, smooth fronds, toothed ones, feathery ones, red and brown and green and yellow. Mary knew about flower-arranging: it was one of her mother's talents – on every speech or sports day she filled the whole school with enormous bowls of flowers. It was not, unfortunately, one of Mary's, hard though her mother had tried to make it so. But she could recognize a good arrangement when she saw one, and besides, these had the advantage that the fronds of seaweed looked almost alive, waving, flowing in the ebb and flow of the sea. She wondered if her mother might achieve the same effect with an electric fan. She would suggest it, she thought, next time the occasion arose.

William, however, was more interested in shells than in seaweed. Suddenly she noticed him bent over sand, sometimes picking a shell out of the pattern, examining it closely before returning it carefully to its place.

'Are you looking for another shell like yours?' she asked.

'Not exactly.' She would have asked him what he meant but at that moment felt a tap on the arm and turned to find a male fish – a very delicately green one – bowing to her, one fin across the place where his heart would have been had he been human.

'Madam,' he was saying, 'may I have the pleasure of this dance?'

Mary looked at him doubtfully and with embarrassment. For one thing he was less than half her size. For another, dancing was one more thing she happened definitely not to be good at, at the best of times. And here underwater, the fishes gyrating above her head looked as much like skaters as dancers, executing turns and complicated steps with slight and easy bends of tails and bodies, a skilful flicking of fins in the strictest tempo.

'Oh, come on, Mary,' urged William, as she hesitated. 'Come on – dance – *try* . . .'

So she nodded her head and tried to dance. To her relief the music almost immediately changed to rock and roll, a hollow-voiced, echoing singer going 'Dooby dooby dooby do, how I love you, Peggy Sue,' and sounding as if he was singing at the bottom of a bath; as well he might do here, she thought. Her own fish pirouetted elegantly round her, turned somersaults, dived beneath her, and came up again but seemed quite satisfied with the vague and out-of-time jiggling that was all Mary could contrive – but few of the lady-fish did much else as far as she could see, even if they looked neater about it than she felt. The chief difficulty was when her fish tried to catch her by the hand and spin her round. All the other pairs touched fins, pushed, and spun successfully like that. But she was handicapped by having an arm and hand instead, useful appendages as a rule, but inconveniently long and clumsy here. They both misjudged it several times and missed each other. And when she at last, infuriated by this, made a grab at his fin and caught him, he was not expecting it, and they collided instead of spinning; which was why, perhaps, when the music stopped, the fish bowed to her again and took himself away.

Mary went back to William, who was laughing uncontrollably.

'That's right, all you wanted was a chance to laugh,' she said crossly. But in a moment she had begun to laugh too; and there seemed to be far more laughing in her than she knew about, because she could not stop – trying to, she clutched at William so clumsily that both of them fell on to the sand, making the water near them slap against the cave walls, setting the decorative seaweed in its turn to wave and bend more furiously than ever. Mary only stopped laughing, and then abruptly, when she saw a pair of sky-blue tail fins just by her, simultaneously heard a voice, sounding indignant, some way above her head.

'You may well laugh,' it said, 'well and indeed you may ...'

She nudged William, who was still lying on his back with his eyes shut, no longer laughing but smiling gently to himself; and they both sat up and stared at what appeared to be an exceedingly academic fish with glasses and shaggy, disordered fins, a large book tucked under each upper one.

'The indignity – of such garments—' He pointed at his own bow tie, somewhat stained and very unevenly tied, at the apron on the lady-fish foxtrotting past. 'Not only crude but stereotyped. Are you in any way responsible for this?'

'Of course not,' said William, indignantly.

'We're only visitors,' said Mary, and added more gently because, though ludicrous, he did seem genuinely upset, 'I'm sorry, we never thought of it like that. I wish we could do something.'

'If wishes were horses,' said the fish, and sighed, grown suddenly more melancholy than angry. 'It's those colours we've been given, you know, so common and unnatural: pink, mauve, *pistachio* ... Ice-cream colours, you might say – not fit for a noble creature like the fish.'

'Nice in ice-creams though,' said William.

'Ice-*creams*? That you *lick*? With tongues? Such vulgar, dionysic eating habits you humans have. Fish and chips for instance ...' The fish closed its eyes slowly and opened them again, dropped one of its books, picked that up, dropped spectacles, and retrieving those, dropped another book. Mary handed it back this time, and he took it without thanking her.

'It all goes to show that only fish are civilized. I should not care to sample, say, boy and chips.'

'You mightn't,' put in William, 'but other fish do. Sharks, for instance. A friend of my father's was eaten by a shark.'

'If that is true – and doubtless you exaggerate ...'

'It's quite true. My father's a marine biologist.'

'*If* it is true, his fate was a noble one. The art of the chase has been hallowed by tradition, also time. There are no vulgarities; no oil, no batter, no fry-up, no vinegar, no tartare sauce, no—' (here he closed his eyes and opened them, began to turn purple instead of blue, and shuddered with a violent quivering of fins) – 'no *ketchup*. Your true fish, like myself, is a creature of the most delicate taste and refinement. Come, I will show you.'

Curious rather than obedient, they followed him round a large rock and found that it blocked the entrance to a smaller cave, by the look of it a kind of retiring room for more senior fish. Some sat round small baize tables playing cards; far more, however, were gathered at a much larger table on which stood an old-fashioned gramophone with a huge horn. They looked intent, appeared to be listening closely.

'As you will have observed,' their fish was saying, 'we have all fallen victims to your human talk, coarse and common as it is. By contrast I would ask you to listen closely ...'

But at first they heard nothing, nothing at all. They did not in any case know what they were supposed to be listening for, and among the murmur of voices – talking unmistakably coarse human talk – it was hard to tell what sounds if any were issuing from the great black curly horn.

'But *listen*—' said their guide imperiously. And now, gradually, they did begin to distinguish sounds – extraordinary unearthly squeaks and moans and groanings, magnified by the echoes from both rock and water, expanding all about them as if they or it were contained within a hollow shell, fading a little, then rising again impressively, despite having underneath it the hiss and scratch of the gramophone needle on an obviously ancient record.

After a little while it came to an end. Strains of rock music leaked in from the bigger cave, and even here several small and evidently very young fish were jigging surreptitiously in corners.

The blue fish frowned in their direction, then turned to William and Mary.

'What was it? What was that noise?' asked Mary, for he appeared to be waiting for them to speak.

'*Noise?* That noise, as you called it, was none other than the ancient dialect of the herring in its purest, undiluted form. Is that not so, ladies and gentlemen?'

The fishes gathered round the gramophone stood motionless, with eyes closed and rapt expressions.

'But what was it saying?' William asked. No one answered him. They were sighing in chorus, shaking their heads.

'Play it again ... let us hear it again.' And so once more came the indecipherable sounds. And again William insisted, 'But whatever does it *mean*?'

This time the blue fish answered him. 'It says nothing, means nothing. The ancient dialects have no saying, are only sounds.'

'But if you don't understand what it means ...'

'Who needs meaning? What can sounds not tell you as much and better? The rhythm, the cadence, the subtly graduated echo ... Alas, alas, that not one of us can speak it now.'

'It's a dead language then, is it? Like Latin or Greek.'

'Like *what* did you say ...?'

'I said it's like Latin and Greek to us – that we learn at school.'

'You said something else ...'

'Dead language.' Mary was being helpful, or so she thought, mistakenly, for the blue fish drew itself up, puffed itself out.

'*Dead?*' it repeated, ominously.

'Yes, dead,' said William firmly. The record ended as he spoke. The word rang out loudly, echoed, diminished only gradually – 'dead, dead, and dead' – and now the fishes were repeating it, louder and louder, angrier and angrier.

'You call our language dead?' the professor said. They had all risen from their tables, were advancing, far more fish than there had looked to be at first; and though individually none was large, most less than half the size of either William or Mary, collectively they looked formidable. Once-feathery fins had developed dangerous-looking spikes, others opened their mouths to show rows of efficient teeth (for us and chips, muttered William to Mary). Their ice-cream colours, their aprons and ties and eyelashes looked suddenly much more threatening than funny.

'Insult!' they were shouting. 'Blasphemy.'

'I think,' said William coolly, 'it's time we were getting out of here. Come on, Mary,' he urged her. Mary moved leaden limbs and found after all they came easily. They both swam out of the small cave, furiously pursued by the angry mob; but as soon as they saw the dancers again in the larger one, still gyrating unconcernedly to the St Louis Blues, William touched Mary's hand with the shell. She felt the spiralling sensations in her head, closed her eyes, then opened them again to the stills, the cinema, and the grey and chilly street.

chapter five

'What did you say your father was?' Mary asked on their way home.

'A marine biologist.'

'What's a marine biologist?'

'Someone who studies life in the sea – plants, fishes, and so on.'

'Does he tell you about it?'

'No doubt he would if he was around. But he isn't usually.'

She was going to ask William what he meant by that. But then thought perhaps she was being too inquisitive. She said, 'Do you mind me asking, William? You can't ask me much. You know all about the school already.'

'I just adore talking about myself,' said William, quite straight-faced. Mary decided he was lying anyway. 'Go on, ask away,' he said, but that effectively drove away any questions. After a minute he began to talk about the weather with exaggerated shivers. 'It's so cold, you wouldn't think it was going to be the summer term soon. The trees hardly have buds on them even.'

'It's always behindhand here,' said Mary. And it was true. If you went inland now, beyond the downs, it would be like another country, with a little film of coming green, where here was all iron greyness, except blossom on some trees, and small brave gatherings of daffodils in corners. 'The spring is always later here,' she said, and wondered why they were so polite to each other, so formal, talking about the weather as if they were grown-up. But William was like that sometimes and made her like it too. It was strange because what they had just experienced ought to have made them nearer, like one person; it had been so ludicrous in some respects, yet quite extraordinary, outside the experience of the world. But it did not. They were as separate as ever, needing to talk like strangers.

*

Next morning she was taken shopping to buy clothes for the summer term. It was another wintry day, and the cotton dresses tried on for size felt comfortless, a thin and chilly skin after her woollen skirt and sweater. But she managed to persuade her mother to buy her a Peanuts T-shirt – there were no plain ones – and her mother, in a hurry as usual, gave in almost at once to Mary's pleas, saying only, 'But you're not to wear it, mind, till the weather's warmer.'

Opposite that shop was the Olde Lanterne Teashoppe where Mary had been given tea occasionally on her mother's rare more leisurely days. But now, suddenly, she thought she saw a distorted face peer out of it imploringly – was startled for a moment, then, separately, afraid – but the distortion was in the thick glass bubble at the centre of a windowpane. When they had crossed the street, it resolved itself into an ordinary and quite untroubled face belonging to a lady in a red hat who sat eating shortbread at the table nearest the window, flanked by rows of craggy home-made cakes set out on wire trays.

At home, despite her mother, she put on the T-shirt, chilly as it was, and went to find William and show it off to him. She could not find him immediately. He was in the woodwork room with its clean wood and bitter resin smell, at the farthest end of the building. He had made a box out of plywood for his shell – a very neat and professional job, cut out with a fretsaw and then glued, each one of its corners dead true.

'It should be lined with something rich and rare,' she said.

'Have you got something rich and rare then?'

'My mother's got a whole drawer of bits. There might be velvet or silk – they'd do. But it ought to be painted too. Shall I paint it, or do you want to?' ventured Mary after a long pause; for, suddenly shy, she had been summoning up the courage to suggest it to him.

'If you want to. If you like. Is it lunchtime yet, Mary? The clock's stopped in here.'

'They always stop them in the holidays. I don't know why. They only have to set them again for termtime.'

'Then is it lunchtime?'

'Oh, no, not nearly.'

'Would we have time to go to the beach and back?'

'I should think so, if we hurry.'

'How about the shell? Shall I leave it here, in its box?'

'Oh, no, please *don't*,' said Mary, and then realized he was, as usual, teasing her, his face though, as usual, expressionless.

The clouds had gone higher, and patches of sunlight showed now and then. But though the sea looked less rough, more quick, choppy, than spread with wide and heaving rollers, the wind seemed sharp as ever. The brightness when it happened was brilliant but steely, making steely glints on the angled surfaces of waves. The wind bit like steel too. Mary regretted the thin T-shirt beneath her coat – William had not even noticed it.

They had come out later than yesterday, and the tide was later also. The sea reached right up to the sea wall, slapped it, retreated, occasionally put small paws over the top with a rush of spray, withdrawing them almost immediately, playfully. They walked up as far as the pier and peered through its locked and rusty gates at the dilapidated kiosks and seats lacking most of their slats. The boards looked rotten, stained different shades of grey and brown, and several were splintered as if feet had gone through them. There were traces of posters on the kiosks, shadows of bright colours, and below the sea complained with echoing, melancholy sounds that made Mary melancholy too for a moment, perhaps William also. Neither of them spoke.

'Why did they close it?' he asked at last.

'It was falling down and not enough people used it. There was quite a fuss though, letters in the paper, things like that.'

'A pity. I like piers.'

'So do I. But there's still one at Brighton,' she added, after a minute.

'Let's go there one day.'

'They'd have to take us. They'd never let us go alone.'

'We wouldn't ask. We needn't tell them.'

'But . . .'

'There's a bus, isn't there? We could get there in an afternoon. We will then. One afternoon. Is this place always so empty?' William asked a moment later. 'I mean in the holidays.'

'Yes always. Even in the summer holidays no one ever comes.'

The town was full of boarding schools. In the roads at the back of it, higher up, where all the big houses mostly stood, every second house was a school with a name like Sea View Preparatory or Grange Lodge. In the holidays it seemed wholly deserted there – huge empty houses, huge empty gardens, and miles and miles of playing fields with nothing in them but goal posts or cricket nets, and possibly a long way off some solitary man mowing grass or marking out pitches with white paint. Mary was glad their school stood right in the town, nearer to the sea, even though it did mean their games field was ten minutes' walk away.

'My father says this is a ghost town in the holidays,' she said. 'But up there on the hill it's so empty I doubt if there are even any ghosts.'

'I'm hungry,' William said suddenly. 'I'm *starving*. It's this air. It's called ozone, did you know? Very good for us. That's why all the schools are here, poor us. What are you going to do about it, Mary, my absolutely raging hunger?'

'Go home, I should think. It's lunchtime soon.'

'I'm hungry *now*. Have you any money?'

'I might have tenpence. Yes, I have.'

'That's enough for crisps. Let's go to the Martello Café.'

Mary had been afraid of that; had she been cleverer, she thought, or a better liar, she would have denied the tenpence. But she could not have explained why she did not want to go there, the reasons were so vague and intangible. William might just think she was afraid, because in termtime the Café was sternly out of bounds.

But they were lucky at first. They ran all the way and found a boy behind the counter instead of Mrs Trent and the Café quite empty otherwise. It was only a café of sorts; it had just four tables surrounded by chairs so flimsy they looked hardly strong enough to carry children. And there was little to buy – the counters and the shelves behind it were almost empty except for some cellophane packets of barley sugar and three sticks of rock, one of them broken. There was also a turning stand for postcards, rather faded, with views of the town, or else highly coloured and having jokes about large fat women and small thin men, which Mary found funny, but which her parents, she knew, would think quite unsuitable. When William asked for two packets of cheese-and-onion-flavoured crisps, the boy produced some ordinary-flavoured ones from a box under the counter and said that was all he had.

'Shall we stay and eat them here?'

'On the way home, or we'll be late for lunch.' But that was not exactly what Mary was afraid of; all she wanted now was to remove herself from here as quickly as possible. Too late, however, for William, walking out of the door, almost knocked over Mrs Trent, who was walking in.

chapter six

'Oh, it's you, Mary lovey,' she said. 'I haven't seen you for quite a while.' She had a low, thick, buried kind of voice. Round her neck was slung a tape measure and a pair of metal-rimmed spectacles on a thin cord. 'I expect you've just been busy then,' she said.

Mary felt her face heat up. She stared at the floor, rather than Mrs Trent, and mumbled to explain the thing to William.

'She lives upstairs; Mrs Trent, I mean. I mean this is Mrs Trent.'

'In the Martello Tower?' asked William.

'In the Martello Tower, my duck,' agreed Mrs Trent. It was actually why Mary knew her. For as long as she could remember she had looked up at the tower with its net-curtained windows and wondered who could be so lucky as to live up there. And also, why the windows needed curtaining, since no one could conceivably peer in, and why there were five doors spaced round the top of the tower, yet all of them opening on to empty air? Then, about a year ago she had gone into the Café to buy an ice-cream (not so much because she actually wanted an ice-cream, as because she had made a point during those holidays of breaking every one in the lengthy list of school rules) and in a moment of courage asked Mrs Trent, then serving her, who lived up above.

'I do, none other,' she had said. 'Would you like to come up, dearie, have a look?' And though at once Mary had felt uneasy – knowing her parents would disapprove, yet also uncomfortably uncertain what they disapproved of – her curiosity had overcome her doubts. In any case her fears proved groundless – Mrs Trent had given her strong tea and the same yellow cake that she sold in the Café downstairs, then sent her home again. There had been nothing to fear or doubt in the whole year since then that Mary had known her. Mrs Trent just looked and sounded, just was, a rather down-at-heel and faintly grubby old woman with sagging clothes and straight grey hair, cut rather crookedly and held back by a slide like a child's. Perhaps she did not wash either her clothes or herself quite as often as Mary was used to in adults approved by her parents; perhaps a sudden sharpness of eye she showed was disconcerting; or the wheedling note in her voice – how about just one more piece of cake she might say, like a gipsy woman trying to persuade you to have your fortune told – followed sometimes, startlingly, by a sudden noisy laugh. At any rate Mary's unease remained. And if one reason for it, her parents' likely disapproval, was a part of the attraction, the unease had been strong enough eventually, once the novelty of Mrs Trent's living quarters had worn off a little, to keep Mary away from the tower entirely.

'You come up and let me show your friend, duck,' Mrs Trent was urging Mary now. 'At once if you like. Yes,' – (only she pronounced it 'Yace') – 'yes, why not. I can lock up here, there'll be no one in over dinnertime. You can have a cup of tea with me and be home in time for yours.'

'Yes, *please*,' William said, before Mary could think up any reason for escape – her first, that they should be late getting home having been so neatly set aside. He had already finished his crisps. He crumbled up the pack and threw it hard at the litter basket. It went in neatly, fell to the bottom, without touching or even just glancing off the wire sides. 'Wow,' he said and smiled. Mary contemplated trying to do the same but decided she would be bound to miss. Besides she still had some crisps left, and there was no point in wasting them. She ate them then and there, waiting for Mrs Trent to lock the door behind them, then dropped the packet into the basket as they passed it.

Despite being perched in mid-air, Mrs Trent's lower room felt almost underground, like a burrow, perhaps, rather than a cave, because padded, cushiony, and smelling of must, paraffin, mothballs, and other things pleasant or not that Mary could never exactly place. The net curtains let in little light and no view of the sea to speak of. Though Mary had never seen her with a customer, Mrs Trent was a dressmaker when not minding the Café downstairs – hence the tape measure and the pins stuck invariably along the pocket of her cardigan like fortifications. Hence all the impedimenta of her trade – an old-fashioned sewing-machine, enamelled black and gold, set on a table so huge it took up most of the floor space; two dressmaker's dummies, both of stout customers evidently; pins in and out of pincushions; packets of needles; cotton reels, full and empty; thimbles; paper patterns – interspersed with ornaments on every surface, including the green table-cloth, while on all the chairs, on backs, seats, arms, if they had them, were piled rolls of cloth, some still tightly rolled, others tumbled; and everywhere, scattered, were snippets of different-coloured cloth.

'I never noticed the seashells,' said Mary so loudly and suddenly she startled herself. But she had simply not taken them in before. They sat on the mantelpiece, about ten of them, jumbled with ornaments and sewing things. William went across immediately to see.

'Interested in shells are you, dovie?' inquired Mrs Trent, watching him, having to shout across the radio on the table beside her, playing a tune that Mary vaguely knew.

'No,' William said. Then, 'Yes.' And to Mary's utter astonishment he took the shell out of his pocket and quite coolly handed it over. Mary suddenly did not want to watch Mrs Trent feel and peer at it. She went to the mantelpiece, squeezing round the outskirts of the table, and examined the shells there carefully instead. They were more exotic than William's shell, yet somehow less interesting. There were huge, pale spiky ones, smoother, shinier, freckled ones, the open sides rather like mouths without faces, Mary thought, because their curling upper lips were lined with indentations like little teeth. There was a long brittle razor shell, and also, hidden among the bigger shells and the sewing things, a number of small coloured shiny cowrie shells.

She had her back to Mrs Trent and William, but looking up saw them reflected in the mirror that hung over the mantelpiece. Mrs Trent had put on her metal-framed spectacles, was holding the lamp, tilting it towards her so that she could look at the shell more closely. For a moment she held it up against the light. Even from here Mary saw how transparent it was, how it seemed to shed a soft and pinkish glow. The rest of the room looked quite different, reflected – as dark and crowded, but strange and sinister besides, even jungle-like, as if unseen life was lurking in corners.

'There's a pair, you know,' she heard Mrs Trent say. 'They come in pairs these, like cockle shells, you can see. There ought to be another one, oughtn't there, dearie?'

'Yes, I know,' William said. But he had not told Mary. She felt a small sharp rise of pain and jealousy, which at once subsided. She was fingering the spikes on the biggest shell, listening to them carefully.

'Would you like to have the other one, my duck?'

'You haven't got it?' William asked in a voice as nearly excited as Mary had ever heard from him.

'Of course not, dearie. How should I? It's at the bottom of the sea somewhere no doubt. Is it worth something to you?'

'Nothing much. I was just interested.' William sounded as cool again as usual.

'Is that so, my dove? Is that all it is?'

'Well, I mean I'd like to find it. It doesn't matter really if I don't.' But it did matter, Mary thought. So that was why he had poked about the seabed yesterday, what he had been looking for. She wished he had told her.

'I see, I see it. Yes,' said Mrs Trent. And then in almost another voice, 'Well, I'll be brewing the tea now. Why don't you take your friend upstairs now, Mary duck, show him the view while you're waiting.'

It was like coming out into the open air after the suffocating room downstairs. Even here there was a slightly stale smell with an overtone rather mysteriously of caraway seeds, but nothing compared to the other one. This room, painted white though not recently, appeared taller too, and despite more evidence of Mrs Trent's profession – more rolls of cloth, another dummy – it looked relatively empty, the space swallowing objects, so that nothing mattered, only sea and sky. It was by far the best room Mary knew, shabby as it was, semicircular, with four windows on the round side, two of them actually doors, but locked – she had tried them – and all looking out upon the sea. With the tide high, apart from the headland there was no land to be seen at all. It was as much like being in a ship as a house, the wind battering, the gulls floating past giving an impression that it moved across the water like a ship till you could feel the very heave and drop of waves beneath your feet.

William liked it too, obviously. He went and pressed his nose to the glass and peered out. The sun appeared from behind a racing cloud, smiled, lit them briefly, before disappearing behind another. For that moment the sea reflected wave patterns on the ceiling above them; and then the patterns, like the light, went out.

'It's not bad at all,' William said, turning back to look at her, his nose pink from being pressed against the glass.

'What do you mean, not *bad*?'

'If it had an engine, it would set sail.'

'Taking the Café and the paving stones? Um. I wonder...'

'A very original ship, like Noah's ark. But I doubt if it would float.'

'With you for Noah, I suppose, and Mrs Trent for Mrs Noah? But then what should I be?'

But Mrs Trent called them now and, reluctant, Mary especially, they clattered down the wooden stairs that were not quite a ladder but not quite a proper staircase either, to find a blue enamel teapot and a plate of very soft digestive biscuits set on a table among the sewing things.

'We'll get a mouthful of pins if we're not careful,' William said very softly when Mrs Trent had gone to fetch cups and sugar, but she returned sooner than expected and might have heard him. At any rate she looked at him hard while William stared back unblinking. Then he smiled at her and Mrs Trent smiled too, very broadly, revealing over-white and even teeth. Well, at least thank goodness she's got them in today, thought Mary, who had once been greeted by a toothless Mrs Trent showing quite pink and empty gums and had not cared for that experience.

But while Mrs Trent and Mary sat at the table with cups of strong sweet tea still too hot to drink, William seemed restless. He roamed round the edges of the room, returning now and then to sip his own tea and put the cup down again. And so it was William who found beneath a stack of old paper patterns another stack of older 78-speed gramophone records and besides these a veneered wooden box that Mary remembered, though it had never occurred to her to wonder what it was, assuming, if anything, it held more of Mrs Trent's sewing things.

'A wind-up gramophone,' said William, opening it. 'You wouldn't mind, would you, if I played something?'

'It's not as good as ...' Mary was about to say 'the horned one', but suddenly remembered where she had seen that and stopped herself hastily.

'Take your pick, duck,' said Mrs Trent between sips of tea. Mary got up to look too, squeezing herself along the narrow space behind the table.

'Can you work it?'

'Yes, of course, we have one at home. My mother collects 78s.' He was taking the handle out of its slot below the turntable, fitting it into a socket at the side, then winding vigorously.

'Turn the radio down,' he said to Mary. 'We won't be able to hear it otherwise.'

'Can I?' Mary looked round at Mrs Trent, who smiled across her teacup and said, 'Help yourself, dovie,' so Mary bent across and reduced a bellow to a thready whisper. Then she returned to William and the gramophone.

He had unfolded the needle arm from its slot and set it ready. He had taken a record from the top of the pile, was about to set it on the turntable.

'What is it?' asked Mary. He peered at the label for a moment. 'Some kind of fishing song, I think.'

'Ah, yes; very jolly, very merry, that,' said Mrs Trent.

William placed the needle on the record carefully. All they heard at first was a scratching noise, and next beneath that, an accordion, joined by voices almost immediately. It was, as Mrs Trent said, a very jolly song. The clock on the mantelpiece struck one, first the note, then its lingering echo.

Neither William nor Mary expected anything; William seemed wholly bewildered, astonished, when Mary looked at him. Nevertheless, he had taken out the shell and now touched her hand with it. The jolly voices continued echoing round her, went from a major key to a strangely wavering minor one, the same voices, yet not the same voices, hollower. She did not know if she had shut her eyes or not; yet the dark, opaque greens of the room became paler, luminous, moved about her, flashed and glittered, and the song came powerfully, then faded, came back again, shortening or lengthening notes randomly echoing, no longer jolly; sinister.

chapter seven

She was frightened but not wholly with her own fear. Some of it came from outside her as much as from within, because she was not alone, far from it. She was surrounded by an enormous school of fish – swimming with them, part of them, part also of their fear. Indeed for one moment she even thought she was a fish but then caught sight, reassuringly, of her ordinary pink hands and felt her independent legs and feet behind her, which meant she did not have a fish's tail.

The fish did not threaten her in any case; did not even

seem aware of her; were only concerned with their flight through the sounding flashing water, green and blue and silver water, green and blue and silver fish, which fish, which water, often hard to tell. All she could be sure of was the eyes about her; thousands and thousands and thousands of unseeing eyes, terrified.

For the flight was in vain, the net inescapable. It rose ahead of them, closed beneath them, drove in behind them, until Mary did not swim any more herself, was rather dragged along, the bodies of the fish enveloping her. She managed to pull her hands up somehow to her face, to her eyes especially, to protect them from the sharp and desperate fins; then broke blindingly into light at last as the trawl net full of fish was heaved over the side of a fishing boat and dumped, jarringly, with a thud on deck.

The net was loosened instantly. The fish began to thrash so furiously she was hard put to protect herself. One leg was entangled in the harsh and tarry meshes of the net, but as best she could she rolled over and pressed her face downwards against the deck, lay there dazed, aching, buffeted.

The singing had ended, if singing there had really been. She could hear – indeed, rather feel right through her – the putter of an engine underneath them, mighty creakings too as if chains were being hauled across the deck. But the flailings and thrashings of the fish lessened after a little while. She began to feel as if she could breathe at last. The air had become her proper element again, as much as she could get at air, that is, for fish. Their stench choked her. Their scales looked vast, the size of dinner plates. They were coarser than she would have expected and uncomfortably bright from where she lay. She struggled energetically, pushed herself up between them, and broke out into space again – only to find herself gazing into an enormous, but human, face; a mouth big enough to eat her, eyes like the saucer-eyes of the dog in the tinder-box story; a giant, it seemed to her, terrified. Only it was not, any more than the fish had been abnormal-sized. It was she who had got smaller, had considerably shrunk.

Quite when she had realized that – quite how she had realized it – amid such terror and confusion, she did not know. It did not make her any the less terrified, to understand what had happened; and certainly it did nothing to protect her now from the enormous hand that reached out and down from the enormous body, pushed the fish aside with such enviable and astonishing ease, and then grabbed her round the waist and swung her up and up, a terrifying distance from the deck. At the same time the man let out a great sound from his opening mouth; she thought at first this must be an enraged, furious roar; then decided it was normal human speech; only, from her reduced size, it appeared so huge she had not been able to decipher it.

She was too frightened of falling to struggle much; but not William, whom she saw suddenly several feet away wriggling vigorously, held by two hands as huge as the one that was holding her. The skin on all the hands was so harsh and rough, so wrinkled and gnarled on this massive scale, it looked like crocodile or dinosaur, perhaps, rather than human skin; while the clothes the men wore, their yellow oilskins, were as awkward and unyielding as the armour of shellfish, cracking loudly each time they moved their arms; cracking now as they raised their captives, peering at them more closely than ever, discussing them. So close their eyes were like windows – only you could not look inside – Mary found herself reflected rather bulbously, as in a convex mirror. Their still more cavernous, lethally-armoured mouths, meanwhile, went on opening and closing; the sounds they made, if louder still from here, began to seem persistent suddenly. Mary at last found she could distinguish words.

'Can you speak?' her captor was demanding, over and over. She almost answered yes, but saw William shaking his head at her and so made no reply.

'What are we going to do with them?' she thought she gathered next. She could barely follow the discussion that followed, but the upshot of it was that she and William were set down at last, to her relief, on the deck behind the wheelhouse, beside a neatly coiled rope, while a huge cane basket was upturned over them, caging them. The men departed then with thunderous footsteps, but one reappeared carrying a slice of bread and an eggcup full of water, which he set carefully beside them before replacing the basket and once again departing.

William began to laugh. 'I suppose they must think we're hungry,' he said. And then, 'Mary, do you suppose they saw you'd got Peanuts on your T-shirt? Whatever can they have thought we *were*?'

'You can laugh,' said Mary indignantly. She ignored the bread. Even if she had been hungry, it would hardly have invited her; at such a size it looked more like a bit of rock than food, rather eroded, and the crust probably too tough for her minute hands to break in any case. But she leaned over the edge of the eggcup and lapped up water with her tongue, as a dog does, only less efficiently. She found herself trembling all over violently, gasping every now and then. It was as if it was not till now that she'd realized, precisely, how terrified she'd been. The effort of drinking calmed her a little. As for William, he still did not seem perturbed at all.

'Fat lot of use this'll do them,' he said.

'What will?'

'Shutting us up in here. We can go whenever we want. With my shell.'

'I hope we can. I think we should go soon.' She could hear the engine still and the clanking sounds and squeaks and creakings. She could hear also a curious slapping sound, repeated over and over.

'Whatever are they doing? Whatever is that noise?' she asked.

'Sorting out fish, I should think.' And yes, she thought, it did sound like bodies, thumped down into the fish hold, one upon another, though the wheelhouse still held both men and fish from view.

She shivered. 'At least we're still alive. At least no one will try to eat us,' she said.

'Goodness, Mary, you do stink of fish.'

'It's not surprising. So do you.' She had been trying to brush some of the huge scales off, but they clung obstinately, and when she looked at William, he too glittered, rather like a fish himself. She sat down on the coil of rope and stared at her tiny feet braced against the enormously grained and knotted deck. William was trying to see if he could squeeze between the cane bars of the basket, in vain, for small as he was, the bars were narrower still.

'We're much bigger than insects,' he said, coming to sit beside her. 'If the world seems so big to us, think what it must seem like to them.'

'I don't even like being this size,' said Mary. Indeed the vastness of everything, as it grew familiar, yet oppressed her more. She too now went to the edge of their prison and peered out, gripping the bars with both her hands. Between here and the stern of the boat, as it swung up and down on the blue-green glittery sea, looked as long as a football pitch, and it was cluttered monstrously with obstacles to their going: ropes, buckets, boxes, each casting a monstrous shadow. How could they escape men who could cross it in two strides, kicking everything aside that hindered them? Especially when beyond the deck there was only sea.

'If we could get out, it wouldn't help,' she said. 'We couldn't possibly escape.' They had to shout at each other, they had always to shout at each other here, their tiny voices having to compete with the relatively vaster sounds of the boat itself, of the water, and the wind.

'I told you. It doesn't matter. We've got the shell,' said William. 'Look, I hadn't dropped it, I don't quite know how. I told you we could go.'

'Well, let's go then,' she said with relief. '*Quick!* I've had enough of this' – and she reached out her hand, but too eagerly, too quickly. The shell had shrunk with them. Touching it, she knocked it out of William's hands, and it fell towards the deck, bounced against the bars, and fell on to the open deck outside their cage, leaving them standing there, staring at each other in dismay and horror – not restored after all to their proper size and place as they had meant to be, but here still under the same cold and empty sky, in the same huge, expanded world.

William was on his hands and knees at once, reaching out. But his fingers barely touched the shell, only succeeded if anything in pushing it further away. Mary tried too, but they both knew it was useless before she started – she was smaller than he, her arm shorter. Anyway, suddenly, she gave a great shriek and dragged at William's arm and leapt back herself.

'Whatever is the matter, Mary?'

'Look!' she said. '*Look* ...' For there it was – and not just one, she saw two of them, and then across the deck another, skittering sideways on long legs, with waving claws and extended eyes – crabs, small ones as crabs go, undeniably, but not small to them. One scrunch of one claw, Mary thought, and her arm would be gone, or a leg or her very neck.

'They'll get in here.' She was crying with fright, clinging to William.

'No they won't. They're too big. Don't get in such a state, Mary. It's all right, really.'

'Except we'll never get away. We'll be stuck like this for ever. We can't possibly get your shell now. How can we? Even if we could reach it.'

'They must come up in the nets with the fish.' William was eyeing the crabs more with interest than anything else. 'Look, there's another one. He's bigger, but I shouldn't think any of them would be worth eating.'

'They'd eat us. What are we going to do?'

'I don't know. I wish I did. We could try singing, I suppose.'

'*Singing.*'

'That tune. The one that got us here ...'

'But we haven't got the shell ...'

'Well, there's nothing else. Sing, Mary.'

'I don't know the tune. I can't sing. You try.'

'I can't sing either.' And from the few notes he produced then, the truth of that was obvious. So she began to search in her head for the tune, the effort calming her rather, holding her mind, preventing her from thinking such frightening thoughts. She went on with it, quite enthusiastically even, and found odd notes and cadences slowly coming back.

'Was it like this?' she asked.

'A little, yes. Well done, Mary. Go on.'

But she could not do much more in the end than hum a line or two; and it was all in vain, nothing changed, they sat in their cage, and the crabs scuttled about and eyed them, and they eyed the crabs and looked at the sky and stamped the deck and sighed with frustration.

So Mary went on singing anyway. She could remember no more of the fishing song than those notes she had already tried. So she sang the songs they learned in school singing classes instead: 'Wrap me up in my tarpaulin jacket', 'There is a tavern in the town', 'Poor old Joe', 'Barbara Allen', starting a new one each time she'd sung all the words she remembered of the last. William joined in occasionally – more of an uneven hum than actual tune – but Mary could not stop, why she did not know unless it was to keep the world out, away from her, and by such frail means too, her only protection this tiny voice caught by the wind and blown away at once, quenched by the other sounds of the boat and its engine and the wind itself.

She had just taken a deep breath and begun, 'On Friday morn, when we set sail, the ship not far from land ...' when the deck began to shiver. And there were footsteps. She looked round in terror, gripped the bars fiercely, and sang on, regardless of William who had to seize her arm and shake her before he could make her hear. 'Shut *up*, Mary, shut *up*. Wait. Watch me. I've an idea and it's the only chance.' So Mary, her mouth still open for the unsung next note, watched and waited, wondering what he was going to do, quite numb herself, with fear and bewilderment. She watched the corner of the deckhouse, and a shadow came round it and then a darker shadow which turned out to be solid, a foot, falling, converging on them. For a terrible moment she thought it would crush the shell. William was there at the point nearest where the shell lay, clutching the bars, crouched, as if ready to spring, but Mary still could not imagine what he meant to do, watching him and it as if in a dream; yet knowing immediately it happened how obvious it was, that it was their only hope, the only thing they could do. The basket was lifted from them. Instantly the man reached down to grab one in either hand, and as instantly William had jumped forward far enough to grab the shell, from under the man's very feet it looked. One jump forward, one back, that was all it took, and he was holding the shell out to Mary. And as the hand reached her, she reached the shell.

The man above her head was humming a familiar tune; so familiar she began to hum it, too, to herself, closing her eyes as she did so. The music filled out, grew, an accordion backing added, the phrases succeeding each other neatly, in tune now, and with several voices singing it, the sound overlaid by the hissing of a record. From a clock the stroke of one was dying as it had died before. She opened her eyes. They were standing in Mrs Trent's front room. So small, so close it was, and they back to human size, so warm after the icy wind and sky, it felt like being buried alive. Mrs Trent herself appeared totally oblivious, sipping her tea and looking at them with a small, incurious, cosying smile.

The record ended then, and Mary said with a sudden shriek, realizing only then what the clock had been telling her, 'Heavens, one o'clock, we'll be late for lunch!' and they had left quickly, clutching half-eaten biscuits, as Mrs Trent insisted they should not leave them, at the same time urging them to return again. But they dropped the biscuits in the litter bin as they rushed past, on top of their own discarded crisps bags, and arrived back a quarter of an hour late, to due opprobrium. Moreover, Mary had her T-shirt confiscated for the time being, because she had worn it when told not to and quite forgotten to remove it.

chapter eight

'Whatever do you think those men thought when we vanished?'

'Perhaps we didn't,' said William. 'Perhaps we're still there as well.'

'They must have thought they'd dreamed it. Or thought they were seeing things. No one would have believed them if they'd told. It must have been a shock. Just think.'

'It can't have been more than the shock it was for us.'

'It was lucky we didn't go on stinking of fish,' said Mary, for the smell of fish had faded to a shadow as the stroke of one died; had gone altogether by the time they reached home.

'Don't you think it was interesting, Mary? That it worked with music. The shell, I mean. Not a picture for once.'

'It was sea music, though, wasn't it?'

'I wonder if it would work with other music.'

'William, do you think it would work with anything to do with the sea? I mean books or poems and things too?'

'What sort of books?'

'Well, there's *Treasure Island*.'

At this William groaned. 'Oh, *no*, not *that*,' he said. 'We've had that read to us every single term.'

'How about *Kon Tiki*?'

'We've had that every other term.'

'All right. You think of something then.'

'I think poems might be better. There are sea poems – there's one about Dunwich ...'

'What's that when it's at home?'

'A place in Suffolk. I went to it once with my mother. Only it isn't there. The sea ate the coast, and it's under the sea now.'

'Like Atlantis.'

'In a way. But different. There's a poem, you see. We had a poetry book with that in, last term. I wonder if I've still got it.'

William's classroom was the highest. Even in the holidays Mary had a guilty feeling going there, as if she was trespassing on the mighty. Not that she let this stop her visiting it, as she did every other room, and even sitting grandly at the head-boy's desk. But now, with William, she hovered by the door in a quite embarrassed way, waiting to be invited in.

'Oh, for heaven's sake,' said William, in an exasperated voice. 'Why can't you ever come properly into rooms? You'll have to help me look for that poem, anyway. The book's not in my desk, but someone else might have it.'

Each desk that Mary opened was a little private world. All had been left tidy at the end of term, but it was easy to tell, even so, which owner was naturally tidy and which was not. For some desks contained tidy books, undecorated and having straight lines and smooth angles, also capped felt pens and rows of pencils with sharp points in pencil cases. But in others the edges of the books were dog-eared and inkstained, the covers drawn on, while the pencils were broken and chewed at the ends and the felt pens lacked tops. Some desks had models of cars or tanks or aeroplanes; some – tidy desks mostly – had pocket chess sets; several had comics folded up and pushed well out of sight. But all alike seemed to shout their owners' names and beings into the silence of the empty classroom, making an expectancy, a feeling that something was about to happen, though it never did, a feeling Mary was used to in the holidays. She rather enjoyed it.

She almost forgot now that she was supposed to be searching for anything in particular, yet recognized the book at once when her eye fell on it, lying in one of the moderately tidy desks under a pile of papers that had compass patterns drawn on them, filled in by felt pens. 'That's it.' William came over and took the book from her as she was flicking through it. He found the poem at once and handed it back to her.

'I like the bits about treading the steeples and the bells ringing under water,' she said, when she had read it through. 'But it's about the land as much as about the sea. And people cooking.'

'Let's try it anyway.' William took the book back and started to read the poem out, rather loudly and rather fast, holding the shell in his other hand. But nothing happened. There was not the kind of hollow, the echo in the air, that came when the shell was about to work.

'Well, I'm not sure I wanted it to work anyway. I'd rather go to Atlantis,' said Mary. 'Are there any poems about Atlantis, do you think?'

'But we've been to Atlantis.'

'Not now it's underwater. Though I suppose if the Dunwich poem didn't work then an Atlantis poem mightn't work either.'

'I wonder. We've never been able to use the shell twice in the same day, do you realize, Mary? Perhaps we can't. Perhaps we'd get to Dunwich if we tried tomorrow.'

'Or perhaps the shell just doesn't work with poems. Anyway, I'd still rather go to Atlantis.'

'Mary, you are nothing if not one-track minded.'

'I'm *not*. I just . . .'

'I'm only teasing, Mary, don't look so upset.'

'I am not a bit upset.'

'All right then, if you can find a poem about Atlantis . . .'

'There isn't one here; I've looked. Only "full fathom five" – you know – "of his bones are coral made".'

' "Those are pearls that were his eyes." Shakespeare,' William said.

'I *know*. Actually, William, even if we could find a poem, I'm not sure I haven't had enough for one day. Haven't you?'

'I never have enough. Yes, you could be right. We could try another picture just to see, but I don't think anything would work in any case. I feel it. We've had our allowance for today.'

' "The dragon-green, the luminous, the serpent-haunted sea," ' Mary was saying softly to herself.

'The serpent-haunted ... whatever's that?'

'It's just another poem here. Not about Atlantis though.'

'Well, watch it. I'd be a bit worried about the serpent-haunting myself.'

'What do you suppose a sea-serpent would be like?'

'Huge, I should think. Vast. Like the pictures of the Loch Ness monster.'

'Yes, I suppose we should be careful.'

*

The sky had clouded over totally by now. The room became very dark and gloomy. The wind and rain were battering the windows, making their iron frames rattle loudly. They had retreated to the art room, because Mary wanted to paint the box William had made for his shell, and now they turned on all the lights in there. Mary fetched her radio, too, at William's suggestion, though when it came he mocked the music every now and then and did a silly dance to it.

'Who gave you the transistor?' he asked suddenly.

'My father did.'

'You must be joking.'

'No, he really did.' But it was about the most astonishing thing her father had ever done, he who forbade transistors in the school, and lectured the boys periodically on the inferiority of pop music. They did have a family radio. Mary had used sometimes to play it to herself, but whenever her mother appeared, she was made to turn it off. And always there were arguments, the worst arguments that Mary and her mother ever had, for some reason. Her father had appeared once in the middle of a particularly violent one to find Mary standing with clenched fists and her eyes shut and tears pouring down her cheeks, yelling out, 'You never let me have anything *I* like.' He had spoken very sternly then, told her never to speak to her mother in such a way, sent her to her room. But next day he had called her to his study and presented her with the transistor, saying, in effect, if she had to have that awful music there it was, and no doubt she would grow out of it. Meanwhile she was not to annoy her mother or anyone else by playing it too loudly in their earshot.

She had not known what to say. What could he mean by this, hating the music as he did? She had taken the transistor gratefully, even hugged him in her surprise and delight, but he had merely said he had work to do, rather stiffly, and sent her away at once.

Today she hardly noticed the music though, except as a wall that shut her from the world outside. She liked paint. She felt she could control it a little, as she could not control flowers for instance, when arranging them under her mother's eye. William roamed round restlessly at first, rather the way he had roamed round Mrs Trent's room that morning; though here there could have been nothing with which he was not entirely familiar; the jars with paint dried on the bottom; the paint-stained drawing boards; the stacking steel chairs and folded trestle tables; even the pictures pinned to boards all round the room and rarely if ever changed – on some the paper was yellowed by now. 'G. Johnson and F. Campbell who did these must be twenty at least by now, if not *fifty*,' said William, peering at a snow scene and another, a Guy Fawkes scene. There were more recent snow and bonfire scenes, too, and seaside and Christmas ones, subjects set by the art master. The others, far more, were chosen by the boys themselves: football here and there, but above all, endlessly, scenes of war – tanks firing guns, aeroplanes dropping bombs, struggling armies, besieged forts, assaulted castles. William peered at each of them but suddenly gave up roaming, found a large white sheet of paper, and began drawing patterns all over it.

'More fish,' Mary said, coming to lean over his shoulder.

'I've got fish on the brain at the moment, swimming about in it literally. It's not surprising. If my head was transparent, you'd see,' he said.

'Thank goodness it isn't,' Mary said.

'Have you finished the box?'

'Almost. I'll touch it up a little when the paint's quite dry.' She brought it out from behind her back and held it out to him. She had painted it a deep sea-green colour all over, then made pictures on the lid; fishes again and seaweed, reddish and yellow, like the seaweed in the underwater cave.

'It won't last. It's only poster-colour,' she said.

'Never mind. It's just right *now*; very appropriate; thank you, Mary.'

'Don't mention it.'

'But I shall mention, Madam, what I like.' And William bowed to her half-solemnly, making Mary giggle a little, confusedly, not knowing how to answer that.

She sat herself up on the windowsill, first removing two

stained and crumpled rags, a small model of a horse's skeleton, a jar full of paintbrushes, and a very old book on the painter called Raphael, with dim and yellowed plates. The window felt cold against her back. The weather drummed at her vainly, could not reach her, met only glass.

William continued to make his patterns, his straight fair hair dropping over his eyes. Two-thirds of the paper was underwater, with the fishes and other underwater things, but the top third was air, and he had drawn ships along it, little ones, sailing boats and steamers – no gun-boats anyway – and among them also small bright flying fish.

Mary thought of his father as she watched him work. 'His work must be very interesting,' she ventured, after a little while.

'Whose work?'

'Your father's. Doesn't he ever tell you about it?'

'Sometimes, when I see him. But he's been on some scientific ship in the Pacific for most of the last two years.'

He answered so easily. It was all so easy and friendly, almost cosy, with the beat of the rain enclosing them, the echo of the radio, the warm lights, and the heat of the small electric fire she had found and switched on for them. Caution did not enter her mind at all.

'The shell must be a Pacific one then,' she said. 'Did he tell you anything about it?'

'Only that there should be another one to make the pair. He said why didn't I look for it.'

'But how could . . .'

'It had to be a joke, of course.' Even so, William had not taken it as a joke. She knew that. It was odd because he took more things as jokes than most people.

'Is that why you had to come here in the holidays? Because your parents are abroad?'

'Yes.'

'But you don't usually come back to school. Where do you go then?'

'I don't need to go anywhere. I stay with my mother.'

Mary knew suddenly, too late, on what dangerous ground she had ventured. She watched William draw an aeroplane in the sky above his fish. He drew it very carefully. Then he drew bombs falling down from it, bright-coloured, decorated bombs, but bombs for all that. Grown cold and sad, how she hardly knew, she would have asked no more. But William answered the hovering questions without them being asked.

'It so happens my parents are separated. My mother has flown out to see my father now to discuss what's to be done; what's going to happen to me, among other things. It had to be now, in the holidays, so I came here. That's all there is to it.'

'I didn't mean to be nosy.' Mary, wretched, looked away from him, out of the window, through cold glass to grey rain and a cold grey sea.

'No one ever means to be nosy,' William said. She felt him look up then; he was staring at her, and at last she too had to turn round, to find him, astonishingly, smiling at her too, a most rare, sweet smile that confused her utterly. Only she found herself, joyfully, smiling back.

'I'm the product of a broken home,' William was saying. 'It sounds like a house taken to pieces by a giant. But we've got a lodger.'

'Whatever are you talking about?' She was almost indignant. It was such a turnabout and so irrelevant.

'He sleeps up under the roof, so there has to be a roof, proof of a whole house,' said William. And he had drawn wings on the bombs and turned them into birds.

chapter nine

It was sunny next morning. Mary woke up early and, seeing the sun, climbed out and opened the window, then went back to bed.

She had forgotten, as you always do in winter, how the outside world invades through open windows. The sounds of cars in the street, the cries of gulls entered and seemed more noisy and immediate than anything in the room itself, her own movements, for instance, pulling the blankets round her.

The gulls floated through her picture as usual. But

there was also a strange flashing among them, persistent enough to make her curious after a while as to what could possibly be making it – an orange spark, on, off, on, off, rapidly – and so she got out of bed again and leaned out of the window in her nightdress to see, just along the street, a yellow van belonging to the electricity board, from which a man had been hoisted to mend one of the street lamps. A warning light on the van roof spun round throwing out the orange sparkles that reflected first on to the street lamp opposite and from here into her own window, making the reflected reflection she had seen.

'Hullo, Mary,' said a voice. She was startled out of her life, craned up uncomfortably, and saw William peering from the window above her head. 'What are you doing there?' she asked indignantly. 'That's not your room.'

'No, but I went to the loo and saw the flashing from the window, only it's frosted, I couldn't see what made it. So I came here next door.'

'Well, don't fall out, will you?'

'I could say the same to you. I do not intend to. You know what, Mary, I've found an Atlantis poem.'

'So have I,' she said, annoyed because she had wanted to find one for herself, then sighed. 'Well, no, not really, bother it. Shall we try yours then after breakfast?'

'We'll go to the beach. We'll try it there,' he said.

The day was still as brilliant then. Each small piece of gravel that the waves had thrown up on to the front had its own small shadow pointed towards the beach, and the sea was a deep rich blue, richer and greener in the shadows, the sun flashing unevenly off the tops of the choppy waves, so brightly sometimes you could not look at them. The sky that had been quite empty earlier now contained little fluffy, fleeing clouds. They threw small, swift shadows across the sea, but none was big enough to hide the sun more than momentarily.

By mutual, if unspoken consent, William and Mary had kept to the far end of the beach from the Martello Tower. After a while they sat down against a support of one of the breakwaters, a whole tree trunk bleached and smoothed by the action of the sea and warm now under the sun. William, his face screwed up against the strong light, seemed in no hurry to produce the Atlantis poem. Mary was determined not to ask for it and did not feel much sense of urgency herself this morning; at least she decided she was not going to let herself feel impatient and did not find it hard to keep to that.

'There's lots of people out today,' William said at last. And, indeed, some of the beach huts were opened and people sat outside them wrapped in rugs like mummies, raising their faces to the sun.

'Term starts next week. There's always more people now.'

'So we've only got five more days to do it in,' said William.

'Five more days to do what?'

'Find my shell, of course.'

'I hadn't noticed us looking much yet, anyway. Till yesterday I didn't even know we were looking – that *you* were looking.'

'I know. That's just the point.'

'Where on earth do we *start* to look?'

'There were shells in that cave we went into. After the film. I looked, but none of them were like mine.'

'But . . . I *say*, William, do you suppose that's why your shell works for you, so that you can look for the other half of it, wherever we go to?'

William looked at her in silence for a moment. Then, very hard and suddenly, he thumped her on the back. 'Mary, you're brilliant. And I never thought.'

'Didn't you?' She was nonchalant as he was ordinarily,

but really very pleased. She said, 'We'd better choose where we go then pretty carefully. Only to places we might find it.'

'We were going to try Atlantis today.'

'And we should still. It's under the sea – there'll be shells. We might as well start there.' She made herself sound as persuasive as possible; shell or no shell, she did not want William to change his mind; she did want to go to Atlantis so very badly. '*Have* you got the poem?' she asked.

'Of course, I thought you were never going to ask.'

> '"Long ago it sunk in the sea
> And now a thousand fathoms deep . . ."'

She was reading to herself now, rather than William, the wind catching the words and blowing them round her. Halfway through, she put out her hand and found the shell, and it all happened as before, except that this time she found herself alone, without William.

*

Again it was hard to realize that she was actually beneath the sea, because again she was breathing water as easily as she would normally breathe air, as if she had gills like a fish instead of nose and mouth. Lying there, alone, she had time to enjoy it, this time. She could feel little rather pleasurable ebbings and flowings round her as her breath went in and out. She discovered that by shaping her mouth she could make bubbles of different sizes – even, very simple patterns with the bubbles – something you could never simply do by breathing air, except a little perhaps on frosty mornings. And this so fascinated and amused her that for a while she forgot to be worried about William's absence.

Still, bit by bit, the silence began to impose itself. She stood up then and began to look about her in the dim green light. There were blocks of tumbled stone nearby and pillars, some lying flat, some half-upright, leaning. But it was hard to tell their shapes exactly. Distorted by water, there looked to be bends in them where none were, solid pieces of stone appearing to bend and shake as if in an earthquake. Indeed, nothing was exactly as it seemed to Mary's eyes. When she reached out a hand to touch one block, it had to stretch further than she expected before meeting stone. She almost overbalanced then, would have done so altogether if water had not held her more strongly than air. As it was she had to put out the other hand to save herself, so found herself hugging the block, rather than touching it. It was marble but very rough in places, elsewhere slippery with plant growth, not at all like the smooth, even marble of the other Atlantis. But then this Atlantis had been under the sea two thousand years at least, and possibly much longer. She did not find she altogether liked that thought.

After a moment, firmly, she pulled herself together, let go the stone, and began to wander. It was hard at first, because she was walking, or trying to, against the pull of the water. Soon she began to swim and found the water helped her now, rather than hindered her. It was as much like flying as like swimming, water being the element she breathed. With a flick of hands or feet she soared, slid through it, then perhaps was caught by currents she could not see, and glided, with another flick of ankle or wrist would shoot upwards again – further perhaps than she intended, pillars of the sunken city falling far beneath. Then she would have to reverse the movement, push herself downward, heaving mightily against the water's apparent pushing-up, back down towards the stone remains, among which surely, somewhere, must be William.

She found herself flying among fishes after a little while, small ones that tickled her face, larger ones also, though as quick to flick away from her. Once she caught sight of something much bigger. A huge and sinister shadow it made, and in a moment of panic she turned and sped the other way. When she dared look back again, the shadow had disappeared, but so also had the shoals of smaller fish. It was now, suddenly, that she began to feel lonely, more lonely than she could possibly endure. There were faces carved on pillars that swung at her out of dark corners, revealed briefly by a shifting of weed or a movement of water. But these were not company, these were worse than being alone. They were broken, sad faces carved so long ago and now so eroded that the features were only dimly visible. Sometimes she saw, but momentarily, in a sideways, accidental glance, that there was a face. Then her eyes rebelled and showed her only simple, if misshapen, stone.

'William!' Mary called. 'William!' But her voice too was distorted and boomed and whispered in the wrong places, so that the echo, returning to her, sounded quite different, did not make the name William at all. She created a whirlpool in the water by spinning round, still shouting, and the echoes filled the water about her – unearthly sounds, not like any human voice.

She grabbed hold of herself, stopped, let the echoes subside, and the water fall as still as it would ever fall. For she could not still everything, not her own breathing, let alone the fishes or those other movements of which she could not tell the origins. But she let the water's greenness and coolness calm her. The water felt silky. She began to rest in it.

Then she saw William. He was bent over, not far away at all, but between two pillars, which must have been what prevented her seeing him before. He was searching, not in the haphazard kind of way she would have searched, but methodically, patch by patch, turning over the silt on the seabed. She glided towards him, put a hand on his shoulders, asked, in a mixture of annoyance and relief, 'Where did *you* get to?'

He had not heard her come. He spun round, and his voice sounded curious, both fuller and yet thinner underwater, as if there were several notes in it at once. 'Oh, there you are. I wondered where you'd got to.'

'I've been hunting *everywhere*,' she said.

'I wasn't worried. I saw you sometimes, I wasn't ever very far away.'

'You might have showed yourself. I thought ... No sign of your shell, I suppose?' she asked him then.

'Not a sign.'

'I'd better help you look, I think.'

But it seemed quite hopeless, even before she started. There was so much on the seabed, so much seabed, come to that, stretching as far as she could see and littered with stones and sand and shed things of all varieties – shed by what exactly or why, it was impossible to tell – the contents might have been sucked out by some predator, or the owner might have grown too large for its outer covering, so cast it off deliberately. At any rate there were shells in abundance, and how you could hope to be lucky enough to happen on one like William's, let alone its actual partner, she did not know. 'If seven maids with seven mops swept up for half a year ...' came floating into her mind; what she was doing seemed no less insuperable a task. But whenever she looked across at William, he was pressing on so doggedly she felt obliged to do the same.

There was flat stone often here, not far beneath the sand; the remains of floors and pavements, obviously. Sometimes it was so near the surface she could scrape the sand away with her hands and reveal it. Mostly it turned out to be plain marble, like the pillars, but once or twice she found patterns, mosaics even, forming pictures, though she could never uncover enough to see what they depicted exactly; finding little odd things, however, that intrigued her, fishes sometimes, appropriately, and once a rather curious plumed bird. Small crabs scuttled across the stone close by her hands; on the jumbled stones around were other signs of life – little peculiar creatures whirling tentacles or fronds. She did not mind them, or the fishes, or any of the other signs of life. She began to find the patterns, though, made so long ago by those long dead, decidedly uncomfortable. Even with William quite close by she began to feel horribly lonely again. And so when he came over to her at last and said, 'It's no good. I think we'd better stop,' at the same time as being disappointed for him she was thankful for herself, joyful even, to find herself back at last under the full and welcoming sun on the beach beside the breakwater.

*

William, she guessed, must be very disappointed. But he did not apparently intend to show it. He smiled at her, putting the shell back in its box and into his pocket, where it made an angular-looking bulge. He started to pick up pebbles and throw them idly at gulls. Then he asked, 'Did you get to see the bones?'

'What bones? No, I did not, how *horrible*.' Though sneakingly, she rather wished she had.

'They were tidy bones. They were very tidy people in Atlantis.'

'I'm still glad I didn't see them.' For now she remembered the man who had talked to them when they went into the picture and found it worried her – bones might be one thing, she thought, but particular bones were quite another. She heard William recite very slowly and softly,

'"Full fathom five thy father lies;
Of his bones are coral made."

Except they weren't,' he said.

Mary had remembered the last two lines of the same poem and recited them to prove it.

> '"Sea-nymphs hourly ring his knell;
> Hark! now I hear them, ding, dong bell."

What do you suppose sea-nymphs would be like, William?'

'They'd be green, I should think, like the water, to camouflage them. Or perhaps they'd be transparent, like jellified sea.'

'Oh, William, don't be so horrible.'

'And their veins and bones and muscles would be sea plants, petrified.'

'*They* would have coral bones,' said Mary. 'The tidy bones of the tidy men of Atlantis,' she said, reminded, liking the sound of that better than the sense.

chapter ten

It was astonishing how in a single night the world had turned from winter into spring; under the simple influence, it seemed, of a warm sun and a brisk but mild wind. Where buds had not appeared, they looked about to. Where they had not burst, it looked at any moment as if they would; the grass on the wasteland appeared almost lush. Still it remained April, so clouds thickened gradually. And if the sun did not remove the sense of spring, it had removed itself quite firmly by the time they finished lunch, while rain started coming and going in the wind.

Mary was sent down to the kitchen by her mother with a message for Mr Penney, the cook, and William followed her.

During termtime the kitchen was forbidden territory – full of too many people, ceaseless activity and quite extraordinary noise: machines with different rhythms endlessly whirring and clattering. But in the holidays Mr Penney, an ex-naval chef, was alone more often than not, and if he was in a good mood he seemed to welcome Mary's company. Indeed, she spent a lot of time there talking to him, or listening to his endless sagas about the navy; sometimes being allowed to taste things, scraping out mixing-bowls, sometimes actually allowed to help, beating up eggs or chopping apples or whatever else was necessary. For apart from cooking their family meals, he would spend his time stewing enormous amounts of fruit and bottling it, baking cakes and pies and freezing them, making endless jam and marmalade and chutney, which you always knew because of the smell pervading the entire school, particularly warm and rich and sweet if it was jam or marmalade, as rich and sweet if it was chutney, but more peculiar, with unidentifiable spiciness – this a smell Mary never knew if she really liked or not.

Mr Penney made bread, too, for their family. In termtime they ate sliced shop bread like everybody else, but during the holidays there was always Mr Penney's homemade, and the smell of its baking was by far the best of all.

'Your last lot,' he said gloomily. For he was making bread now, kneading it furiously at one end of the enormous table. 'Back to the old sliced next week. But I daresay you'll be pleased to get at the Latin again, Mary,' he said, and winked at both of them.

Mary wondered if he would let them help him knead. But it was no use asking – he would never allow it then.

Mr Penney was altogether rather odd and moody. He looked odd. He had a small head and narrow features, his mouth opening and shutting in a thin line like a turtle's, no matter what he said. But this head was set on the broadest of shoulders: he was in fact a very big and bumbly man, his large, awkward limbs making movements that looked as awkward, but were actually quick and efficient and very silent as he strode about on feet as relatively small compared to the rest of him as was his head, but shod always in whitened, rubber-soled tennis shoes. As for his mood, she never knew exactly how he would greet her, straight-faced or with pleasure or an underlying growl, what he would actually say or do.

But his mood seemed good enough for them today. He told a couple of his stories, both ones Mary had heard several times before. Then, after a little while – and she could tell even by the way he was handling the dough that he was quite likely to – he broke two hunks from it and handed one each to herself and William.

'Mind you treat it rough,' he said. 'It's what dough likes, to be treated rough.'

'It feels alive,' William said. 'It's like flesh. It's lovely.'

'It is alive. Yeast's an animal, it feels what you feel. If you feel bad when you're making it, it'll notice; it won't rise so well.'

'Mine ought to be good then today. I feel brilliant.' And indeed William looked it, Mary thought. And she was surprised because, after their fruitless search this morning, she might have expected him to be gloomy. Only he was not. 'If flesh is like this, I'll have to be a masseur in future life,' he said.

'They'd have to be pretty fat people to feel like this when you massaged them,' said Mary.

'The fatter, the better. Lovely fat, meaty women,' said

William, grinning and slapping away together, punching the dough and pulling it, turning it over and over and over.

'That's quite enough of that, my lad,' said Mr Penney. 'Enough of the dough, too. You don't have to knead it for ever. It's got to prove now.'

He took eight large baking tins from the top of the stove, divided his own dough into four, kneading each piece for a moment quickly, his hands as thick and clumsy-looking as the rest of him, but as neat, as easy – then he set these pieces into four of the tins and showed William and Mary how to divide and set their dough in the others, pressing it into the corners of the tins with their fingers. He put all eight tins back on the warm stove, under the chimney, and covered them with a large damp cloth.

'Right,' he said. 'Now it's time for rosie.' And he made tea in a large tin teapot, pouring it out into the cups and adding milk and a lot of sugar without asking William or Mary if they liked their tea that way, then setting the cups, saucerless, on the table before them.

It was like a room within a room, where they were sitting. Beyond was the huge kitchen in which so many shiny things – saucepans, implements, machines big enough to mix concrete or even metal – reflected such harsh and restless lights. But here between window and stove it was peaceful, another place, no one saying very much, but sipping the hot sweet tea from the cups between their hands, the grain of the table printing itself on their elbows.

Mary watched Mr Penney, thinking as usual, with astonishment, how much he'd seen, how much he'd known, and wondering as uncomprehendingly how so much knowing and seeing and doing could possibly be contained here within their kitchen, within Mr Penney's narrow head: the China Sea and the Pacific; the icy Atlantic in wartime; the sailors gobbling his roasts and his fry-ups, his pies and his puddings, while the gales roared outside or the guns sounded; the typhoons and the tempests and the hurricanes.

It seemed appropriate – she was not at all surprised – when William put his hand in his pocket and pulled out the shell in its box to show to him. But she found she did not like it. She did not like it one little bit.

'That shell come from the Indian Ocean, then?' asked Mr Penney.

'Pacific, I think.'

'Ah, well, they're next to each other. A beauty, isn't it?'

'But there's only half of it.'

'Lucky to have that, aren't you?'

'Yes, of course. But it would be good if we did find the other half as well,' said Mary, who, though angry with William, still found herself wanting to defend him, if Mr Penney was hinting he might be greedy, which she thought he was.

'But that's not likely, is it?' said Mr Penney, looking from one of them to the other and back again.

William put the shell back into its box and back into his pocket. Then, 'Look,' he said, and when they turned they saw the bread had heaved itself up under the damp cloth making eight neatly rounded humps.

'Is it ready?' asked Mary. 'Can I look and see?'

'No need.' And Mr Penney pulled himself out of his chair and had all eight tins inside the hot oven and its door shut and was back drinking tea immediately. It was as peaceful as ever, you could imagine the peace lasting infinitely, none of them shifting, just sitting on and on. And yet it was not unexpected or inappropriate either to find Mr Penney suddenly rising to his feet and indicating 'Out' with both voice and hands, having them quite meekly and obediently on the far side of the kitchen door before they'd caught up with the fact that he was ordering them there. The smell of the baking bread followed them all the way to William's classroom.

'Why did you have to show him the shell?' Mary asked William then, indignantly. 'You show it to everyone.'

'I'll show it to everyone I like if I think it might help.'

'But how could Mr Penney help? How could anyone? You know what he said.'

'Yes, but all the same you never know.'

'Well, I think it was a waste of time.'

'You can think what you like. You can take your thoughts out, frame them, and hang them on the wall if you like. They might look better too. But they still can't make me do anything.' They were standing there, glaring at each other. But then William dropped his hair over his eyes and laughed, and Mary found herself laughing back.

'Oh, William, you are silly.'

'Not at all. Merely logical,' said William, again unsmiling.

*

The science room was a cool, pale, bleakly-lit place, smelling faintly like a hospital. There was a skeleton behind the door, made of plastic 'unfortunately', said William, setting it to swing. There were tall benches made of dark red wood, set with gas taps and Bunsen burners. 'But the gas is turned off in the holidays,' Mary pointed out.

'Well, I wasn't thinking of blowing up the joint today,' said William, perching himself on a tall stool. They were in fact looking for underwater pictures – it had been Mary's idea – for at one end of the room was the science library, so-called, actually six shelves of books, which she now began to go through carefully.

'We'll still be able to go on looking in termtime, you know,' she said.

'No, it would be too late.'
'How do you know?'
'I don't know. I just feel it.'
'Your bones again, I suppose.'
'Yes, my brilliant bones.'
'Anyway if it's you that's in a hurry, you'd better come and help, William. I don't see why I should do all the work.'
'I do. It's delicious. I'm your actual male chauvinist pig.'
'What's that when it's at home?'
'A man who likes watching women work. Among other things.'
'You're not a man yet.'
'I shall be. I'm practising.'
'Well, stop practising. Come and help. I can't find anything.'
And indeed, books about the sea were few and far between – despite one shelf labelled marine life – and what pictures there were tended to be diagrammatic with little labels pointing out the organs of fish or octopi or squid.
'I don't think,' said William, 'there'd be any future in contemplating at close quarters an octopus's beak.'
'Or the gills of a fish for that matter. Have you ever thought, William, some large fish could have swallowed your shell?'
'No, and I don't want to think about it.'
Mary wondered if William thought the task of finding the shell as hopeless, basically, as she had begun to consider it herself. He had left her heap of books and wandered across to the fish tank that stood on a windowsill among jars containing less identifiable, rather sinister things. It was coated with slime inside and a few small goldfish swum lethargically among bright green water weeds.

'How about putting ourselves into that?' he said.

'Do you think we even *could*? Anyway, that wouldn't help find your shell. *Goldfish*. Nothing else.'

But the fish were their excuse to be in the room at all. Even though the gas was turned off and the chemicals safe in a padlocked cupboard, it was the one place where Mary was not allowed to go. Her mother came in each day to feed the fish herself – for some reason Mary could never understand, she refused to keep them in their flat during the holidays. Today, however, rushing around with lists headed dry goods and laundry and looking even more harassed than usual, she had surrendered the key quite willingly when Mary had offered to do the job for her.

'But come out at *once*. And remember to lock the door. You'd better return the key to Miss Pitt's office.' And this they now did, somewhat disconsolate, following the small chatter of the typewriter and knocking on the door from which it came.

Miss Pitt was almost ecstatically pleased to see them. 'Come in. Come in,' she said. 'What a very nice surprise, Mary, *and* William.' Mary was almost as equally ecstatic herself – she had quite forgotten about the clutter of magazines and periodicals for which there was no room elsewhere so were kept in Miss Pitt's office.

'The *National Geographic*s, of *course*,' she said. 'Miss Pitt, please can we look at them, William and me? The *National Geographic* magazines. William, don't you see, they're always having articles about the sea, about under the sea, underwater photographs.' There had been one holiday when it had rained continually, and she had spent most of her time there, in Miss Pitt's office, lying on the floor and looking at the pictures, reading some of the articles too, about anything from whale fishing to the remotest tribes in Borneo. 'William and I are very interested in undersea exploration,' she explained to Miss Pitt now.

'That's very nice, dear, look away.' So look away they did, dragging out piles of magazines wildly (Mary) or systematically (William). No one could have touched them recently because clouds of dust came out, making them both sneeze. 'I do hope you're not getting colds,' Miss Pitt said.

'Look,' Mary said, at last. 'Look, William, I've found it. And it's the Pacific too, the best place for your shell.' It was an article about a coral reef complete with underwater photographs that showed fish of quite dazzling and startling colour and design.

'But they've cheated,' said William. 'They must have cheated, it wouldn't ever really be as bright as that, not unless they used enormous lights.' Some of the pictures, however, explored bluer, dimmer caves and showed men with finned feet and masks and breathing apparatus and carrying three-pronged harpoons much like Neptune's trident.

'Lucky them,' said Mary wistfully, forgetting their own possibilities. And, 'Lucky *us*,' said William, pointing into a photograph that showed no men, only the brilliant fish. And he brought out the shell, and all was as usual, except that this time beneath the sea they had been provided rather disappointingly with breathing apparatus and goggles, with fins on their feet and even, rather unnecessarily, with the three-pronged harpoons. Mary discarded hers almost immediately, because she had no intention of trying to catch any fish, and the thing merely got in her way, catching on coral edges when she tried to swim.

But she did not like any of it much. Goggles impeded her sight to right and left, and the breathing apparatus was uncomfortably heavy, besides making every breath she took extremely noisy and echo-y, releasing behind her a trail of indecently showy bubbles. She much preferred the way she had breathed before, as natural in water as in air –

but when she grabbed William's arm and pointed at her mask and goggles to suggest removing them, he shook his head violently, and she concluded what she really knew quite well already, that if they had been provided with this gear it must mean they needed it, that they would drown without it. It meant too, however, that she and William could not talk to each other; they had to communicate by signs. He was pointing at the seabed now, and she knew that this time he wanted her to start looking for the shell. He began at once himself, still clutching his harpoon, but she wanted more time to take in their surroundings, to explore them. For this was quite, quite, different from Atlantis: not dim at all, rather it shone, it glittered, it felt like being let loose in an enchanting, yet extraordinary jewelled garden. Even the sand seemed to glitter. It was quite brilliantly white. And she did try very hard at first to attend to it, to help William, who moved so steadily, so persistently across the seabed ahead of her, his harpoon also soon discarded. The sand was full of small pebbles, all different colours, shiny and smooth and sometimes almost translucent, of shells of every size and shape and form, pointed or curly, rough or smooth, some, urchin shells, prickly as hedgehogs, and none of them in the least like William's; but it hardly seemed to matter, they were good enough. To Mary, suddenly, it was an enormous open treasure chest and all hers. So for a little while, quite enjoyably, she kept her eyes where she was supposed to.

But gradually – inevitably – she became distracted by everything that was going on around. The light and the water slipped about her, changing endlessly, as air and sunlight does not change. The reef too: it was covered in growth, live corals, seaweeds, sponges, anemones, which plants, which animals, it was impossible to tell, all seemed equally mobile and alive, sucking in water, blowing it out again, moving continuously or seeming to. There were broad fronds, indented, narrow, fleshy or wispy ones, branched corals, tentacled anemones, forests on forests of them. Only the fish, it seemed, were ever still. A single fish or shoal would freeze entirely. Then flick, dart on, and flick once more, dart another way, and then again hang motionless, almost invisible if you did not know where to look. There were shoals of round black fish narrow as coins, with white fins fine as muslin blowing to and fro. There were vividly striped fish, vividly spotted fish, fish with patterns on like paisley, orange and turquoise, glowing or seeming to; thin fish, fat fish, troupes of fish, trios of fish, pairs of fish, solitary fish, all propelling themselves through the water in fluid, ever-changing patterns, and able sometimes to vanish totally against their background. So that sometimes you would think there were no fish anywhere at all, except for some black and white ones, always single, that lay apparently at ease on comfortable-looking, white spongelike plants, exactly as if they were in bed, Mary thought.

She would find herself going to look closer at one or other of the fish. As that darted off, she would catch sight of a second, would be pursuing another, then another, as a cat in a garden chases butterflies. Without realizing it, gradually she had left William a long way behind her. Sometimes she would be peering into coral caves, blue, dim places. She might even venture a little way inside, then retreat hastily, because for all she knew there could be monsters lurking – giant squid, octopi. Were there such creatures here? She did not know but did not want to find out, she decided. So she would leave the indented and curious tunnels and return to her proper task, surveying the bright white sand, turning up shells, many with occupants that resisted her tugging fingers and dug themselves deeper into sand.

She did not hear any sound. If there was any, her

breathing apparatus drowned it. She explored this world through sight and touch only, and that was rich enough – the way it glinted, beckoned, led her on.

She had lost sight of William altogether now. But she did not mind. She was still not at all afraid. The sun was overhead here, its rays penetrating the water, and somehow that seemed reassurance enough. Once, vaguely, she thought of sharks. But the idea went out of her head almost as soon as it came into it; sharks, she thought, liked deeper water, and if she avoided deep caves, avoided scraping her skin on the reef – she vaguely remembered hearing that could be nasty – she felt she was safe enough, and so went on, lured by the fish that flicked past, touching her skin rather pleasantly.

But she came to a gap in the reef. The light was bluer, dimmer here. In the distance she could see another coral arm like the one she had explored, and still feeling strong, indestructible, she swam out between them. She would not go far, just a little way to see; it would not hurt, it could not hurt, and she wanted to see what lay beyond.

But there lay nothing, nothing at all, a great blue, empty void disappearing down into black darkness. She did not like it at all, she almost hated it, but she was drawn down into it all the same; it was as if something was sucking her, pulling her. Quickly, she was deeper than she meant – she had only been idling along till now, but when she kicked, the frog feet gave her a powerful extra thrust. She was almost hurtling down against the push of sea. There was no colour any more. She began to be engulfed by darkness. And suddenly, too, she began to be engulfed by black terror, so she turned upwards, thrust with her feet, upwards and upwards seeking the light, the sun, and still it was not fast enough; she was terrified. And suddenly she saw it, about ten yards or so away it looked.

A wicked-looking shape, with the unmistakable single fin.

A shark. A *shark*. She was so frightened anyway, it almost added nothing to the fear she felt. She did not imagine its vicious teeth. She could not imagine a shark actually eating her. She just stayed still a moment looking at it as if mesmerized and then turned and flicked her feet and gasped into the noisy mask, and kicked and struggled and somehow sped in through the coral arms and across the white seabed, never looking behind her, only ahead to where William still bent patiently, still turning over pebbles and shells. She swam up to him so fast, she almost knocked him over. And only then, clutching him, dared look round. The shark was not there, it had not followed her. But that made no difference, she held him still and gasped; and he, seeing her panic, took the shell and restored them again to Miss Pitt's office, to the magazines and dust and the tapping typewriter, the oblivious Miss Pitt pursing her lips as she gazed at the sheet from which she typed.

'Well, what was it? What was the matter?' he asked, when they had recovered their breath a little, and sighed when she told him.

'You mean it had gone, and you still . . .'

'I was frightened,' she admitted in a small voice. 'And it wasn't just that. There was the nothingness ... it ...' She did not know how to explain it; she was somewhat embarrassed now because of her panic. 'Just water, just a great, black empty hole.'

'So it would be,' said William. 'It's the deep sea there, didn't you know? They're not like England, those islands; they're just huge mountains with tops sticking out of the sea, and coral reefs grown out round them.'

'I didn't know. I'd forgotten. I didn't realize. Oh, William, do you think I stopped you finding your shell?'

'Oh, I expect I'd have found it, or something like it if it had been there,' said William generously. 'And I was getting bored; you could say I was getting bored.'

*

'You showed Miss Pitt your shell. I don't see how that would help us find it; showing Miss Pitt your shell,' Mary said later. But it was a statement this time as much as a complaint. She had not exactly been pleased when, after they had stayed talking to Miss Pitt for a little while, William, leaning nonchalantly against a filing cabinet with his hands in his pockets, had suddenly pulled one of them out with the shell on it. But she had not been surprised either, indeed discovered herself fairly resigned to it on the whole. Perhaps, partly, because she was feeling guilty about her panic.

'What a pretty shell!' Miss Pitt had exclaimed and taken it from William, saying, 'May I?' when the shell was already between her hands.

'It comes from the Pacific,' William had said.

'The sea makes such pretty things. I do so love the sea.'

'Is that why you came here, to live by the sea?' Mary found herself asking. 'Do you like living by the sea, Miss Pitt?' But she had never before thought of Miss Pitt doing anything else, of ever having had a choice, any more than she, Mary, had ever had a choice, who had to remain where her parents were. But Miss Pitt must once have decided to come here, instead of somewhere else; she was a separate person. At which obvious, yet extraordinary thought – about as extraordinary as thinking of her mother deciding to marry someone other than her father – Mary looked at Miss Pitt for a moment in utter astonishment; and then promptly forgot about it, because Miss Pitt was being so familiarly Miss Pittlike.

'I think it is very bracing and healthy, dear. I went on a sea cruise once too, from Gibraltar.'

'Was it good? Did you have any enormous storms?'

'It was very nice. But my digestion did not altogether benefit. And I lost no less than two headscarves, blown overboard, one with pictures on of Sydney harbour, quite new, that my niece in Australia sent.'

*

They got on a bus that afternoon in splendid blowy sunlight and rode out to the Seven Sisters cliffs and walked on the smooth and grey-green grass along the edge, looking at the grey-blue sea below; Mary anxious every time William got too close, though the edge was fenced, but not liking to admit she was anxious. They did not talk about the shell. They did not talk much at all. William had been very silent since the morning, despite having said he did not mind what had happened because of Mary's panic. She wondered now what he was thinking but did not like to ask. They agreed, however, that next day they would go on the bus to Brighton to look at the pier. 'And the aquarium,' Mary said, 'we ought to look at the aquarium. They've got some tanks full of Pacific fish.' Having decided which, they made their way home, full of sun and wind, and played around in the music rooms for the rest of the day, thumping out chopsticks, solos, and duets on each of the pianos there in turn. They shut the doors, but Mary's mother heard them all the same, their chopsticks jangling along hollow passages, and came and scolded them, looking very tired, her hair somewhat unusually dishevelled, her hands full of notebooks and of papers. 'As if I hadn't quite enough to do,' she said.

'She's always like this just before term starts,' Mary said to William apologetically.

'She does work very hard, your mother. My mother . . .' William began but did not finish it.

chapter eleven

Next morning Mary had to help her mother put away their family china. Always at the beginning of every holiday, Mary's mother unpacked it very carefully, washing every cup and plate and saucer in the pantry next door to the dining room, stacking them on the draining board from which Mary took and dried them with equal care. She did not mind that task, indeed she rather enjoyed it. It was a ritual that for her, far more than the packing of trunks, the departure of boys in busloads, signified the end of term while, equally, the repacking of the china in

newspaper and woodshavings from the woodwork room meant the beginning of it, as it did now. She hoped that William had noticed at meals that it was their china they used and not something belonging to the school. At any rate, if he hadn't, he must notice it today, eating lunch off the plain white plates that the school provided instead of their own that had ivy-wreaths all round.

Where William went that morning she did not know and did not ask. But she did not mind as much as she would have ordinarily not being able to go with him, because of the trip to Brighton that afternoon. After lunch they said they were going for a walk again, instead walked only to the centre of the town and caught the bus that followed the switchback road to Brighton. Up they went, over the downs that were blanketed by neat houses with red and green tiled roofs and fancy brickwork, like houses in a toy building set, down into valleys that led out to the sea. In one they crossed a swing bridge over a canal that was lined with familiar-looking fishing boats. 'I wonder if we were on one of those,' Mary said to William rather excitedly, when she noticed them.

They went to the pier first, though they had decided to start with the aquarium. You could say that was the bus's fault, because it stopped right at the entrance to the pier by the sweetshop, which was unlike any other sweetshop either of them had ever seen, too perfect almost to be real, they thought, too highly coloured, like something out of a pantomime set, like Hansel and Gretel's gingerbread house. Striped candy sticks hung all around the walls, above rows of enormous open tins containing pink and white and green sweets wrapped in cellophane. The shelves were heaped with slabs of pink home-made coconut ice with white home-made peppermint and rich brown fudge and yellow butterscotch and transparent bags full of black-and-white striped humbugs. 'The real old-fashioned kind,' said Mary, with satisfaction. They bought a bag of these and a quarter of home-made peanut brittle and wandered out sucking contentedly, paid their five-penny pieces at the turnstile and walked on to the hollow and echoing boards of the pier itself.

Mary loved all of it: the curly ironwork on every pillar, along the edge of every roof, repeating itself in shadow today against the bright white surfaces, the little round stained-glass windows along the central amusement hall with their pictures of ships and windmills and country churches. Though Easter had come and gone, the preparations for summer were not yet finished. There was new white paint everywhere, some of it still in paintpots held by men, perched on ladders, wielding paintbrushes, the smell competing successfully with the sea smell of mud and salt and seaweed, with their own strongly peppermint-scented breath. Some of the kiosks were still blind, empty – 'Whatever are bauble trees?' asked William, pointing at a notice displayed above one of these – and the ones that were open seemed mostly to sell more sweets, but here disguised as eggs and bacon or kippers or sausages or pies or even hamburgers, laid out neatly on paper plates. Mary considered buying William a peppermint kipper as a joke, but decided that twenty pence was rather too expensive for a joke after all, and offered him a piece of peanut brittle to eat instead.

The end of the pier was still closed after the winter. They went as far along it as they were allowed to go and leaned over the railing there and looked at the sea. It failed somehow to catch the light today, despite the strong sun, the wrinkles on it defined by shadows instead of glints. And close in to the pier it changed colour, from blue-green turned brownish-grey, and rolling in beneath gave the impression, almost, that the pier was moving with it, along the tide.

'"Time like an ever-rolling stream",' said Mary, reminded unexpectedly of a hymn they sang at school.

'"Bears all her sons away",' finished William. 'That's us, Mary, the sons being borne away, doesn't it make you feel sad?'

'I'm not a son. I'm a daughter.'

'It doesn't matter. It comes to the same thing. It really means all of us.'

'I suppose it does.' Mary was thinking for the first time, properly, of the holidays sliding away beneath her as the sea slid now – a few days only, and she would not have William to herself any more, maybe he would not want her at all any more. She could not bear to think about it for very long.

'Look at all those men fishing,' she said. 'Don't they look ridiculous.' There was an angling competition. Just a little way away from them, men in dark blue donkey jackets or sombre anoraks stood in a line with rods hung out over the railings and baskets open beside them, all dead serious and utterly silent, not a smile or a sound between them.

'How can they all catch anything, lined up like that?' said William. 'All it does is offer the fish a choice of bait. You'd think even a fish would get suspicious.' Which may not have been funny especially, but made Mary laugh inordinately, and William too, after a little while, watching her. Until at last they ran back up the pier still giggling madly and with thunderous feet, taking surreptitious glances behind them at the solemn anglers, none of whom appeared to have moved a muscle, let alone caught a single fish.

'Have you got some money for the fruit machines, Mary? Let's try and win something if we can.'

The amusement hall was very noisy, full of machines whirring and clattering away (not unlike Mr Penney's kitchen, it occurred to Mary). There even sounded now and then a fanfare of somewhat rusty trumpets, followed immediately by the thud of hooves. It came from a machine holding a model of the Grand National – horses, fences, everything. 'And that is one thing I shall *not* be playing,' said William. But there was almost nothing he could not do instead, shoot down bank robbers or hostile planes, play football, land on the moon, winning money thus with luck, but more likely, losing it. All over the hall people with concentrated faces pulled levers, pushed buttons, turned handles, and the machines went gulp, gulp, GULP, chewing up every coin and only occasionally disgorging some.

Mary was waiting in a queue to get change, wondering which machine she would try first, when William pulled at her arm and said, 'Look! Look who's *here*.'

'Where, where?' she asked, looking about her vaguely, not imagining what he could be going on about.

'There,' said William, 'look, *there*,' and then indeed Mary saw her – Mrs Trent – two machines away, pulling steadily at handles, her face entirely blank, while pineapples, cherries, strawberries succeeded each other vainly in the rows of little windows.

'Duck,' Mary said, 'don't let her see us,' but too late. As if at the sound of her voice, though she could hardly have heard it, Mrs Trent looked up and saw them, looked back at her machine, pulled two more handles, waited, received nothing, then briskly rattled the handles again, and still receiving nothing gave up, and came towards them purposefully.

'Well, it's not my lucky day today,' she said. 'And well, my dovies, fancy seeing you. You're going to try your luck now, are you. Yes. Yes' – (or rather, 'Yace'). 'You never know what chance will bring.'

'Well, actually, we were just about to go to the aquarium,' said Mary, stiffly; who wanted to escape now as quickly as she could.

'Waiting to get some change were you? There's plenty of time yet for everything. You've got a lucky look today Mary; give it to me, my lovies, I'll show you how to do it.'

So they did not play football or attempt to land on the moon. They did not descend the miniature ski-course, trying to avoid the gates by spinning a wheel at the critical moment, nor work the sky gunner, penny falls, the silver strike, the Indianapolis motor race, or even the Super Spooky Shoot. Instructed eagerly by Mrs Trent, they spent all their change on the fruit machines, hoping to get three strawberries, pineapples, cherries – three anything – in a line. Mary won fivepence once but lost it immediately; whatever Mrs Trent urged and continued to urge while the pennies vanished noisily, one by one, it was not her lucky day or William's. But after a while and so long as she had money left, she was infected by it, to her annoyance, and by Mrs Trent's never-fading hopefulness; at the same time growing ever more furious, and showing it, though Mrs Trent appeared to notice nothing. William was laughing at both of them – Mary became even crosser with him eventually than with Mrs Trent and equally cross with the machines because they would not let her win; pulling their handles furiously as if they alone were to blame and because she was able to treat them as roughly as she felt like treating the others and naturally could not. Her last penny gave her a lemon, an orange, and a cherry – worthless. She even considered fetching more change, counting the money in her purse to see if she had enough for her bus fare and the aquarium besides. Then she pushed it back into her pocket, angrily. 'It's no good,' she said. 'No one could win anything on those wretched things,' and strode away, out of the hall, not saying goodbye to Mrs Trent – immediately knowing she should have done, but determined not to go back to do so. She was halfway back down the pier before she even looked round to see if William followed her; then found not only him but Mrs Trent, lumbering awkwardly at his side, both of them talking earnestly and neither apparently aware of Mary.

'It's too much. It's too much. It's spoiling everything ...' Yet the gulls still screamed, the sea was as green and blue as ever. She walked under the filigree arches, their shadows patterning her face, her hands too when she held them out, and she could not help enjoying that, though she was so angry too. When William called her, she ignored him totally. He hurried, however, and caught up with her.

'We thought we should try the hall of crazy mirrors. I might even be gentlemanly and pay for you.'

'You go. I don't want to.'

'Me and Mrs Trent. Just think what we'll look like.'

'I don't know why she has to keep coming with us.'

'She's just a poor old thing. Don't be so mean, Mary.'

'She's not coming to the aquarium with us.'

'She won't. But are you coming now?'

'Do I have to?'

'Naturally, you don't have to. But do, Mary.'

When they walked back together, Mrs Trent was smiling at her as if nothing was the matter. Mary looked away and then reluctantly, with effort, smiled back. Mrs Trent wore a green beret today, but underneath her straight hair was pulled back with a round pink slide. She wore an old macintosh, her black bag bulged and sagged and had a broken clasp that she continually tried to close.

'Suppose I look like that when I'm old,' thought Mary. 'I wonder if I might. I won't let myself, I won't.' But how entirely could you help it? You could not help growing old, for a start.

'Not your lucky day either, dearie, as it turned out,' Mrs Trent was saying. 'Else the luck must be coming to you some other way. You never know, do you? Last time I won a cup of tea and a bun and my bus fare home.'

William was beckoning them from the kiosk at the entrance to the Krazy Mirrors, the tickets in his hand. Mrs Trent looked almost excited about it, to Mary's surprise and infinite embarrassment. She said, 'I haven't hardly been in one of these since I was your age, Mary duck.'

In the hall they were shortened, lengthened, cut in half by mirrors. Mrs Trent laughed at herself roundly every time, no matter how bizarre she looked. William did not smile at all, let alone laugh, gazed at himself entirely solemnly. Mary sometimes laughed out loud, more often half-smiled, half-frowned at what she saw. The different mirrors distorted different parts of her – once she put out her hands and they reared towards her, vast, huge, something other than hands, belonged to her and yet did not, like her own horrible leering mouth or her expanded and bulbous nose elsewhere.

'I should think I look quite bad enough without,' said Mrs Trent, who was still, nevertheless, laughing heartily. 'Give Dracula nightmares, these would.'

'Mm,' said William in Mary's ear. 'I'm not so sure about this.' They were standing in front of a mirror that made their legs very short and squat, as if belonging to dwarves in a circus, but at the same time gave them long thin bodies and brought their heads to a point on top. 'What *do* you look like, Mary?' She was experimenting with her hands and arms, discovered that if she raised them they too grew long and thin, but down close to her sides became stumpy again, like her legs and feet.

'No worse than you, I expect.'

'Think if I really looked like this,' said Mrs Trent,

flapping her bag up and down, the clasp open, but she no longer tried to close it.

'Don't worry, Mary. It is only a reflection.'

'I know. But think of really looking like that ...'

'Freaky. Absolutely freaky. Perhaps we would if we went in, into the mirror, like into pictures. Look like that.'

'*William.*' Mary gazed at him, horrified. Suppose they could go into the mirror images. Suppose they could become their mirror images. Suppose ... suppose ...

They were being teased in other ways now besides. The floor beneath them suddenly tipped and squeaked, and a little further on a gust of cold air blew up their legs lifting Mary's skirt and Mrs Trent's macintosh, while the mirror that followed twisted their bodies like corkscrews.

'I've had enough of this, I've had enough.' Mary was almost panicking.

William looked at her and said, but kindly, 'Cheer up. It's not so bad really. How about a ride on the ghost train next?'

'With all those green skeletons? No, thanks *very* much.' Though she would have much preferred the green skeletons, she thought, to this, the last mirror of all. It made two of each of them, one standing on the other's head – Mary on Mary, William on William, Mrs Trent on Mrs Trent – but all of them squat, distorted, twice over. She was thinking about it still as they emerged, blinking and rather relieved, into the open air and walked up the pier. The thought would not go away.

'We could go in, couldn't we?' she said to William quietly. 'They are pictures really, like anything else?'

'But it's nothing to do with the sea. The shell mightn't work. It's only worked with sea things before.'

'It's on the pier, isn't it? We haven't used the shell today.'

'Do you really mean you'd like to go back in and try?'

'Yes. No. Of course not. Of *course* not.' But not the least creepy thing, Mary thought, was her own curiosity, not to say almost willingness, to try at the same time as finding the idea so perfectly appalling.

'Well, I'm glad. We would hardly be likely to find my shell in mirror pictures of ourselves.'

But still, all the way to the turnstiles, she had this little vivid, horrid picture in her head of all of them shorter and squatter than reality and each with their doubles carried on their heads. And would there only be those Marys and those Williams and those Mrs Trents? Or would their ordinary single selves be facing the selves that the mirror made, making three of each of them? William's stride was very long now. She had to skip to keep up with him. Mrs Trent did not even try.

'Don't wait for me, lovies. Don't wait for me.' But William stopped, and Mary too, who had forgotten her ill-temper now, forgotten to be angry with Mrs Trent. The pictures in the mirror and inside her head had been so much worse that it was almost good to see the real undistorted figure of Mrs Trent coming towards her, one slide, one beret, one shabby bag; so she smiled and asked, 'Would you like a cup of tea, Mrs Trent?' without having been properly aware in advance that she was going to ask it.

They had tea at the Penguin Café in the aquarium – at least Mrs Trent had tea. Both William and Mary had chocolate milkshakes. Afterwards, to Mary's relief, Mrs Trent went off – leaving them to look at their fishes alone was how she put it – though first she bought a comic from the news stand and thrust it into William's hands. 'As a thank-you for being good to me,' she said, making Mary feel a little guilty. The comic was a version of *Twenty*

Thousand Leagues Under the Sea: In Full Colour, it boasted.

'Undersea monsters,' said Mary, 'as if we needed them.' Then she put it into her jacket pocket and forgot all about it.

*

Immediately they entered the aquarium, they could not imagine why they had been so keen to come. Dim and dank, it also smelt sourly of Dettol and chlorine, and its concrete flooring rang hollow like a pavement across the wide and empty hall. The fish tanks were set into the walls – you gazed into them as if through lighted windows. But many of these tanks were empty too. Every now and then there echoed round them a burst of hollow coughing sounds that was seals barking in their nearby pen.

'Whatever made us think we should come here?' asked William.

'Because it's to do with the sea, I suppose,' said Mary. But it did not feel like the sea, it did not smell like it.

They progressed along the windows, one by one. The fish gazed back at Mary as unflinchingly as she gazed at them. Their gills pumping in and out, they remained otherwise quite still – great grey, gawping, spotted fish, other smaller grey ones with markings like chicken wire, still smaller though brighter ones in tropical tanks. Others flicked away and past as indifferent as she felt, because she could hardly take any of it in, wandering blindly from tank to tank to tank, hardly noticing even that one, labelled Kiddies Garden, was more full of plastic gnomes than fish.

'Do you know the seaweed's plastic?' William said once, indignantly. But suddenly he grasped Mary's arm so tight it hurt.

'Look,' he said. '*Look.*' But Mary had been looking already, rather more intently here, because this tank contained a hollow garden, and she recognized with pleasure in this dismal place a number of its occupants – corals, anemones, and fish besides.

'I am looking . . .' she protested now.

'No, there, at the back – don't you notice something?' His voice broke with excitement. But when she looked at him, curious, he stepped back, pushed aside his falling lock of hair, put his hands in his pockets, and said quite coolly, 'I expect it's an illusion, as usual, but I think I can see my shell.'

chapter twelve

Then Mary saw it too, tucked under a rock at the back. And William was right, it could have been the other half of his shell; it was very similar, as far as she could see. A black-and-white-striped, rather familiar-looking fish was nosing there, partially blocking her view of it.

'There's nothing else for it. We'll have to go in and see,' said William.

'Do you think we could? Would the shell work like that?'

'Well, we've got to try, haven't we?'

'But it isn't a picture or a poem or music. It's real.'

'Never mind. We can try. If not, we'll have to think of something else.'

But they did not have to think of anything else after all, because the shell worked at once, very neatly, and there they were breathing water and inside the tank. But – and this they had not expected, though had either of them considered, no doubt they would have realized it was inevitable – they had shrunk, were small again, miniatures of themselves.

The corals were like living trees; the anemones, dangerous man-eating bushes. Even the smallest fishes were the size of cows. Mary clung to William's arm. 'Suppose someone looking in sees us,' she said, and the words echoed through the water, bounced against the glass of the tank, and came back, fragmented.

'Never mind if they do. We can get ourselves out again quicker than they can come.'

Beyond the glass, beyond the brightly lit water in which they moved with the fishes and the corals and anemones, was the darkness of the human aquarium world; huge bodies moved across it; distorted by the water, they seemed to flow like waves, and Mary felt utterly exposed to them, to all those eyes. There were eyes immediately around her too. When a fish nosed at her, she shrank away; and yet felt less threatened by him than by the eyes outside that had not yet noticed her, the hands that could not reach her anyway for glass.

'Come on, Mary,' William urged her. They stumbled round pebbles the size of rocks. It took them a few minutes to locate the shell because perspectives and distances were so different now, and then William only dragged it out with difficulty, for it was, though not very heavy, almost as tall as he.

And this was another difficulty that had never occurred

to Mary. Their eyes were not adjusted to a shell this size, so how could they compare it to the one they held easily between their hands? William's shell having naturally shrunk with them, its grooves and markings were small, their size, not huge, coarse, pitted runnels, as on this other one.

'I think it must be the same kind,' William said at last. 'I think it could be the other half of mine. Don't you think it could be, Mary?'

'It doesn't seem to me quite the same colour,' she said, regretfully. 'It's different, you know, William, it really is.' How strange their voices sounded, booming through the water; she was surprised no one came running to look into their tank to see what it could be.

'I suppose you're right. Bother you, Mary.' But William went on exploring all the same, rubbing his hands over and over it, getting Mary to help him reverse it, so that he could examine the interior, smoother, shinier than the outside, but still coarser to both eye and hand than William's own, the little shell.

Mary had almost forgotten their exposure in the tank, meanwhile – at least standing against the rocks at the back of it she had felt less vulnerable, less dangerously visible, than she had done earlier. But now to her horror, she saw a strange roundish pink shape pressed up against the glass, and with even more horror recognized a human face, flattened by the glass, distorted by the water, with holes in it that were its eyes and mouth and nostrils. And then came more faces, similarly distorted, and behind more bodies pressing, more and more of them, dim but menacing. The faces were like growths. The world outside was like another planet, its inhabitants much stranger, more monstrous than the fish in here that so gently nosed at them.

'William. *William.*' But gently, kindly, he took her hand

and touched it to the shell. The next thing she knew, she was back in the echoing chilly hall, standing amid the group of people gathered at the tank containing the coral garden, pushing and straining at each other's backs, and gabbling excitedly. William was the proper size again, as she was herself, though she touched herself quickly to make quite sure, realizing instantly how silly that was. For how could William appear the right size if she was not that same size again herself?

*

'Well, I got it,' said William, as they climbed up the steps and back into the sun. 'There you are, Mary, a present from the aquarium,' and he dropped the second shell right into her hand. Its markings were darker, as she had said, and it was a little smaller than his own. Yet it was of the same species, unmistakably.

'Still, it's the nearest yet.' He sounded elated. 'It's really encouraging. Perhaps we really have some hope of finding it.'

'I thought you thought we would in any case.'

'Oh, yes, of course. But it's good to have encouragement.' Then he laughed. 'Did you see the keeper, as we came away, come to look for us? He'll think they're all mad. A two-minutes' mass hallucination of you and me. Only it wasn't a hallucination.'

'*Two* minutes, is that all, it felt like hours.'

'We were only in the tank five minutes altogether. I looked at the clock again when we came out.'

'There isn't any time usually, when the shell takes us somewhere.'

'But it's never taken us into a real place before.'

'The coral garden was a real place. In a photograph, of course. But we saw the tank with our own eyes directly. We don't usually, William, do you realize? Someone else has always seen it first and made a picture of it.'

'Sometimes, Mary, you can be quite intelligent. I had honestly never thought of that.'

'You see, sometimes, William, *I've* got brilliant bones. Perhaps we should try the real sea as well.'

'I wonder if we'd dare,' said William, thoughtfully.

*

Mary lay awake that night, clouds and vapours chasing through her mind, interesting apparitions and alarming ones. Lying there in the dark she could still feel how it was to be tiny in an enormous world, arched over by the sky, dwarfed by ordinary things. It was odd yet all the same not totally unpleasant.

But why, oh, why, should this be happening to her? Why the shell? What did it mean? Why, above all, did William want to find its other half, why did he need to? And it came to her with the most utter astonishment that she did not know this at all, she had simply accepted his wish to find it. And now she wondered why. She racked her brain, oh why? oh why?

*

The next morning they had to go to church at half-past nine. Mary was somewhat cross about it – she thought she would have been excused, the last Sunday of the holidays, had William not been there, for whom her mother would feel obliged to set a good example.

'In fact, I never go at home,' said William. 'My mother doesn't believe in God, and I'm not sure I do, actually. Though I have to admit that I quite like singing hymns.'

'Well, I don't. And you use too many words,' said Mary, rather to her own surprise. William's nonchalance irritated her for some reason that morning – maybe it was just because of church.

'I won't speak in future,' William said. It was impossible to tell whether he was amused, annoyed, or neither. Perhaps he simply didn't care. At any rate, almost at once, they went to his classroom, taking Mrs Trent's comic, which Mary had found in her jacket pocket, with its drawings of the Nautilus and of deep-sea monsters – crabs and lobsters and octopi and squid.

'But I could draw better monsters than that,' said William.

'Why don't you try then?' Mary asked.

'Why don't both of us? Tell you what, we could get a long piece of paper and do some sort of frieze. A joint effort. Would you like to?' And since Mary could suggest no alternative – besides, though she did not actually admit it, she liked William's idea – they did just this, using felt pens, the claws and beaks and teeth of William's monsters indeed very fiercesome; while Mary at the far end of the paper drew, for the sake of being different, a large elaborate whale with open jaws and, in spite of it being underwater, an enormous spout.

'Is that whale for Jonah?' William asked.

'I hadn't thought of it. But what a good idea. I'll make sure it's comfortable,' she said; and wrote HOTEL WHALE in large letters across the whale's forehead. But she looked critically at William's monsters. 'Well, this is one picture I don't think we should go into. I don't think I care for them at all,' she said.

'*I* hadn't thought of that. What a fantastic idea, to go into a picture we drew ourselves!' and then, disconsolately, 'I don't suppose it would help us to find my shell.'

'But,' she said, remembering what she had thought last night, '*but*, why do you want to find your shell? Why does it matter, anyway?'

He didn't answer for a moment. And at last, in what was for him a small voice, said, 'I don't think I know. I wish I did.' Which made her angry suddenly.

'You mean all this time? Then it's so silly, William, what's the point of looking when it's so hopeless? We could just have been enjoying ourselves, instead of searching all the time. Unless you do know why and just won't tell me.'

'I don't, I said. And no doubt you're right, it is silly. Perhaps we should stop looking for it altogether.' William began humming to himself, and he drew another octopus with longer tentacles than ever. But when Mary looked at his face, it was suddenly so stricken and unhappy, despite the careless humming, that she was astonished again, and then overcome with contrition; as well as surprised still to find herself attacking him.

'No,' she said gently. 'Let's not stop. Let's go on looking. But, William ...' For there was something lurking at the bottom of her mind, a feeling she had that she could not quite get at but which she thought was important. 'William, do you think we could ever really choose the right place to find it?'

'But what else can we do?'

'I'm not sure that's right.'

'You are such an optimist today, Mary, aren't you?'

'There are so many places we could choose, William ...'

'Well, what do you suggest instead?'

'I think. I think ...' After a long pause in which she was struggling to decipher what she felt, she blurted out, 'I think we might as well trust to luck.'

'But we have to anyway ...'

'I think if we're going to find it, we will. If we're not, we're not. I just feel,' she said rather desperately, 'I just don't see how else it could be.'

'But it's a Pacific shell. So shouldn't we look for it in the Pacific? It was you who said we should choose likely places.'

'William, the Pacific is so *big*.'

'I did know that, actually.'

'It's not an ordinary shell even if it does come from the Pacific. It's not likely to be anywhere ordinary.'

'The Pacific's not ordinary.'

'It would be for a Pacific shell.'

'Do you mean that there needn't be any logic in it? That it's no use looking for it in the logical, obvious place?'

'I suppose that's what I mean. I suppose I mean we just have to let it happen, to take it as it comes, easily.' The thought came easily too, suddenly, straight out of her head, which had felt so muddled up till then.

'Just as you always take things, Mary, I suppose.' But he was teasing.

'Beast,' she said to him, and laughed. And it did not seem to matter any more that she did not know why they had to find the shell.

'Do you know some music called the "*Cathédrale Engloutie*", Mary?'

'The cata *what*?'

'It's French. The sunken cathedral, if you like.'

'I knew it was French. But no, I don't.'

'How about trying that, if I can find the record? If you've got it here. It's most appropriate for Sunday, if nothing else.'

'The Dunwich poem had churches in too,' she said, 'if we can't find it.'

But it wasn't in the collection of records kept with the record player on the platform in the school gymnasium, and William grew very despondent again at this. He hung limply over the parallel bars, his hair flopping over his eyes, while, again, Mary was irritated. She turned three neat somersaults on the wall bars and three more beside William on the parallels; the dark red wood rendered up to her its unmistakable bitter smell and taste – she bit it gently, hung upside down for a moment, and then righted herself, feeling superior. Gym was one of the few things she was actually quite good at, unlike William who was now attempting a slow and awkward roll.

'Cheer up, it's not the end of the world,' she said.

'Being bad at gym? I never thought it was.'

'I meant not being able to find your music. I told you there was the Dunwich poem. About churches, if you want churches.'

'As you pointed out before, it's mostly about Dunwich on land and before the sea swallowed it.'

'Not the churches. Don't you remember the nice bit about the waves treading the spires?'

'I'm sure we wouldn't find the shell just wandering about on land.'

'I thought we weren't going to try to look for your shell any more. You felt like churches – all right, let's try churches. It can't do any harm.'

'I suppose not,' William said, and allowed himself to be led back to his classroom, where they had to search the desks again for the poetry book, since they could not remember in which one they had located it before.

How odd it was, Mary thought as she searched, to find herself for a change telling William what to do. She thought too – or rather realized, with some surprise – how after four days she had come to take his company for granted almost. She had never taken anyone's company for granted before. And how equally strange it was that she should treat it so lightly. Would he want to stay friends, she wondered, once term started? But before she had time to begin worrying about this, she found herself staring at William's own desk, in which in impeccable order were laid out his pens and exercise books and papers. There was the *Observer Book of Sea Life*, besides, and a copy of *The Box of Delights*, a pencil sharpener shaped like a submarine, a small microscope with a set of slides, and underneath the books, when she picked one up, a colour photograph of a man and a woman sitting on a beach. 'Oh,' she said, and would have taken it to view more closely had not William just that moment said, 'I've found it,' and then she slammed the desk shut guiltily, feeling she ought not to be spying on him, especially right beneath his nose. But William did not seem to have noticed, reading from the book held open in his hand.

'I told you, it's not about the sea, so much as land, people cooking. Still if that's really what you want . . .'

'Can you think of something else instead?'

'As a matter of fact, I can't. Inspiration seems to be lacking this morning. Sorry, Mary.' And expressionless, he held out the shell and began to read.

'"Fifteen churches lie here,
Under the North Sea.
Forty-five years ago,
The last went down the cliff . . ."'

And there they were indeed, on the very top of a sandy cliff. It had to be a day in summer because the nettles were high and green, but the wind was bleak all the same and scoured their faces and made Mary's ears ache. Behind them were a few huts and a car park, below them a pebbled beach like their own and the grey sea.

'"Eating the land as it walks,"' said Mary, quoting from the same poem.

'Let's hope it doesn't eat us too,' William said. 'Come on, Mary, there's a path down here; let's go down to the beach.'

The path slipped under their feet, small stones and wisps of sand dislodging themselves, as if the sea had taken a few half-hearted nibbles at it already. There were a few thorn bushes and at the bottom of the cliff a thin belt of sparse, spiky grass on a sand dune, beyond that the shingle and the flat, blank, grey sea.

'You wouldn't think there was a town under it,' said Mary, 'let alone fifteen churches.'

'It wouldn't be close in. It was a long time ago, I think. It would be right far out. I told you ...'

'Then we'll have to go out too,' said Mary. 'How about that boat – we could take that.' But as the enormity of her suggestion – that they should in effect steal the boat – began to sink in, she faltered, 'Well, perhaps ...' appalled at herself, while William, who had been looking rather limp again and helpless, suddenly regained his usual aplomb and confidence and took charge of both of them.

'You're brilliant, Mary, as usual. I can row. Can you?' he asked, and in a while had her and boat – though with considerable efforts of united pull and puff, which at first seemed hopeless – across the few yards of pebbles and into the water.

They took an oar each after a while. The sea was not rough, but, inevitably, it was choppier than it looked from the shore. William had found it hard rowing by himself; the boat tossed and the oars came out unevenly.

'If we both tried ...' Mary had suggested. 'I never have but ...'

'Well, we could try,' William had answered dubiously, but rowing, to her surprise and pleasure, turned out to be something else Mary could do, and after some initial lurchings and awkwardness, their strokes began to match each other and the boat to move more steadily. And in the delight of achieving this – besides the weariness, the hard usage of unaccustomed muscles – she forgot to be afraid that the boat's owner would appear on the beach and yell, 'Stop thief!' after them. In a little while anyway, shouting would have done no good; they were well off shore and there was no other boat in sight that could have followed them.

'I think we make a pretty good combination,' said

William. 'It's exhausting, though. I'll soon have had enough.'

'And me. But what then, William?'

'Listen, I think, Mary. Listen for the bells.'

They drifted, rocked by the water which slapped the boat and talked to itself and them, dipping them sometimes into deeper waves at steeper angles, so that they held the side of the boat for safety. Mary had her oar up out of the water, balanced on the rowlock and the side of the boat. She could feel her hands smarting where the wood had particularly rubbed. The muscles along her back and shoulders ached too but not unpleasantly.

'Better ship it properly, Mary. It would be dire to lose it.'

A gull floated with them, surveying them beadily, rising and falling as they rose and fell. Not a single feather stirred on it, though the wind tossed their human hair about.

'Can't you hear something, Mary?'

She heard wind and she heard water. And then she heard something else, a kind of deep, ringing echo coming and going, so that you thought in the going you had imagined it, and then coming again, there it was, a sound both far away and long ago.

'Fifteen churches, Mary, do you think?'

'And now?' asked Mary, and shut her eyes. At which the whole balance of what she was hearing changed; it was as if she was in a cave, against which the bells echoed hollowly, while the whispering of the water over and under it made now the lesser, if the steadier, sound.

*

And perhaps she slept. Perhaps it was a dream, perhaps it was real. But she felt herself under the sea and wandering the streets of a dim green town. They were recognizable streets, the windows of the houses were full of ghostly presences – she wandered in at doors and out again and seemed to see women bent over fires and cooking pots and men polishing armour or making things; shoemakers, carpenters, blacksmiths, who worked at lathe or bench or anvil with the water flowing dimly round them and the weeds growing up through the floors and fishes swimming here and there. But she went in and out of the churches too; all fifteen of them, she counted, having pointed or round arches, thick pillars or narrow ones, crude and simple decoration or ornate and elaborate; churches so small they were almost like toy churches, large and lofty ones for a whole and wealthy town, with enormous windows and with monuments to wool merchants, whose numerous children were shown kneeling in a descending line behind their upright parents. Each church had its own echo of bells and seemed to contain a phantom congregation, as if the sea itself sang hymns and whispered prayers and listened, sighing, to interminable sermons; as if the very fish in shoals and schools came hurrying to receive salvation.

'Time like an ever-rolling stream,' said Mary to herself, and opened her eyes at last amid the faint echoes of the bells, to the now more loudly creaking boat and the insistent speaking of the water and the wind.

They rowed back in silence. The way seemed twice as long, and Mary did not enjoy the rowing any more; she was too tired, she ached too much, besides being apprehensive in case an angry man should be awaiting them. But the beach remained as empty as when they had first seen it, without even ghostly presences.

'How can you believe so many people lived here once?' she said, as they beached the boat and wearily began to climb the cliff.

'Yet I'm glad we went, aren't you?' asked William, back in their classroom.

'Yes, I am too.'

'Even though there wasn't a shell in sight.' And he smiled, they smiled at each other; and Mary went in to lunch very calm and pleased and happy, all her earlier irritation forgotten, quite unprepared for any blow to come.

chapter thirteen

Not that blow anyway, taking William, as she did, so extraordinarily for granted. She did not even notice at first what her mother was saying over their roast beef and Yorkshire pudding eaten off the white school plates.

'Oh, William, you're going to tea this afternoon with John Dixon in your class.'

'Have I been asked?'

'Well, naturally, dear. His mother rang this morning. I understood you'd told Dixon – John – you would be here. I am sure you would be glad of some male company by now.'

'The male is unimportant, but I should like to see John. I expect you could come too, Mary, if you wanted, but I shouldn't if I were you.'

'But Mary has not been invited in any case. And I am sure she can amuse herself this afternoon. It has been very good of you, William, to keep her company. It is a little lonely for her, you know, in the holidays.'

'Don't mention it.' William bowed a little at both of them, though he smiled at Mary too. But she would not smile back at him and glared at her mother for implying it must be a bore to spend his time with her, making it obvious she had no friends. She felt herself go scarlet with humiliation and with shock and disappointment, and after lunch she went away by herself and did not even say goodbye to William, though he came later and knocked on her door and said goodbye to her, very briefly, removing his head almost as soon as he had put it round the door. Perhaps he had seen her face. Or perhaps, simply, he was in a hurry, whether he had noticed it or not. Either way, clearly he did not intend to involve himself.

So she returned to her usual occupation, lying on her bed, the radio humming away gently. But it did not calm or amuse her today. She just became more and more miserable thinking about it all; more and more convinced that William had actually looked glad to get away from her, then more and more angry because he had not fought for her to come, which meant certainly, she thought, that he had not wanted her to. Odd, hot tears began to course down her face. Finally, she could bear it no more, jumped up, switched off the radio, and went out of her room, slamming the door so that it echoed all over the house. But the passages were empty; everyone, even her mother for once, was inanimate. It was totally forbidden for Mary to disturb either of her parents after lunch on Sunday – and all the rest of the time they're working, she thought to herself bitterly, so when can I talk to them? But anyway, she did not want to talk to anybody now. She roamed everywhere, from woodwork shop to art room, in and out of classrooms, including William's, where their frieze was pinned up on the board that ran along one wall, next to some illustrated essays on the Tutankhamen exhibition. She was so angry at the sight of it, so furiously sad, that she almost tore it down and destroyed it. But then after all, it did not seem worth the effort, so she went out again and on again, ending up at last in the gymnasium under the stage at the farther end. That was where she had used to come to cry when she was younger and unhappy. So here she was again, arrived as if by instinct, because she had almost forgotten it, creeping wretchedly into the little hollow, chilly, dusty place and curling herself up. And now she began to cry again, and having started, found she could not stop, because at a momentary pause the total silence and emptiness oppressed and frightened her. It was like being the only person alive in the world. And she did not want to be the only person – better not to be alive at all, she thought. She curled herself tighter and tighter, as if she could make herself vanish altogether eventually. She remembered seeing conjurors at parties clench up their hands with a single white ball in each, which when they opened them would be gone, squeezed out of existence, so it appeared. That was what she wanted now, to squeeze herself out of existence. Then William wouldn't matter, his shell wouldn't matter. Nothing would matter any more. And at the thought of it, she cried harder than ever, till at last she did not know what she was crying for, only that there was all this crying in her which had to come out. From quiet sobbing, she ended howling aloud, almost enjoyably, although she was at the same time so genuinely wretched.

She was making far too much noise to hear the footsteps, but became conscious suddenly of some difference in the atmosphere and screwed her head round a little and opened her eyes – to find hers looking sideways into those of her father, very startled, his head twisted sideways to see beneath the stage.

'Whatever are you doing, Mary? Whatever is the matter?' But it only made her wail more dismally than ever.

'Come out of there at once, Mary.' And this time his headmaster's voice touched a dim sense in her; she acted automatically, not daring to disobey. But when she had emerged and unbent herself uncomfortably and stood up, she saw that he looked more bewildered than stern or angry. And immediately, she began to cry again. His hand was on her shoulder, shaking it a little, very gently.

'Now then, Mary,' he said, but anxiously.

'Oh, I *wish* I was a boy.' The way it burst out startled even Mary herself; she had not expected to say it, had hardly even known that at that moment she was thinking it. 'Oh, I *wish* I was a boy.'

'Mary, Mary . . .' And the utter amazement in his voice penetrated even her wretchedness and noise, and she looked up to see him holding out a handkerchief to her, which she took and, when she had wiped her eyes with it, found that her crying had ceased more or less, only echoes of her sobs remaining and some odd spasmodic gulps.

'Now then, Mary,' he said after a little while. She had scrubbed her eyes by then and her face. The handkerchief when she looked at it was black with the dust she had picked up from underneath the stage. 'Now then, Mary, tell me what you said.' His voice was calmer again too, more ordinary.

'I said . . .' And she stopped, did not want to go on, was about to defy him; only once more at the sight of his headmaster's face, habit reasserted itself – the awe of his position.

'I said I wished I was a boy,' she said sulkily.

'But *whatever* makes you wish a thing like that?'

'No one wants me because I'm a girl.'

'But I thought William . . . where is William this afternoon?'

'He's gone to tea with a boy. Boys only want to be with other boys, they'll only put up with girls if there's no one else; and I am a girl.' This made her feel so sorry for herself again that she wept a little more, realized how ridiculous it was, though, almost immediately and stopped and mopped at herself with the large and grubby handkerchief. Her father, meanwhile, had touched her shoulder again, then withdrawn his hand.

'It's very cold in here. I think we should continue this discussion in my study, Mary.'

But it was formal in his study, if warmer. He seemed

wholly a headmaster again, and the things Mary had been thinking about, on the verge of saying to him even as they walked back up the stairs and along the passages, vanished back inside her head. He sat her down in an armchair beside the fire, then went to his desk and began looking through some papers, not taking any notice of her or saying anything. The warmth made her realize how cold she had been. In her relief she began to shiver violently but gradually the warmth soaked through, unwound her. She began to feel sleepy, practically cosy, absorbed in watching the movements of the fire. She had almost forgotten her father. He still had not spoken, still sat at the papers on his desk, occasionally frowning and marking something with his black fountain pen. His voice when it came at last made Mary jump.

'Now then, Mary, let's hear some more of this.'

She did not begin well, began, 'Sir ...' hesitantly, and he said quite angrily, 'Don't call me "Sir",' adding quietly, 'I'm not just simply your headmaster, Mary.'

'I know. I didn't mean to. I don't usually.' And indeed she did not. She was meant to call him 'Sir' or 'Mr Passmore' in school, in front of the boys, but was so determined not to, resenting that she should be expected to because he was her father really, that in termtime she never called him anything at all. She did call him 'Daddy' in the holidays. Only it was then, too, that off her guard she forgot sometimes and 'Sir' slipped out unintentionally. But she'd noticed it always annoyed him exceedingly.

She began again, more hesitant that ever, but was in spite of everything so soothed by the fire, by the quiet, and being left alone, that the words began to tumble fairly soon, all very jumbled and confused, so that she did not always know what she was saying herself, and nor by the look of him did her father; and afterwards she could not remember which things she had said and which she had not, and certainly was as surprised herself by a lot of them, because she did not know she had thought so much before, only she supposed she must have, otherwise why did she suddenly start saying them? It was the immediate things at first, about William and his going out to tea and not apparently wanting her to come – though she wondered even as she spoke whether actually this was fair to him, whether she hadn't imagined most of it. Then, more and more, she spoke about the school: about being the only girl, so wishing she was a boy, about being the headmaster's daughter, and people thinking she would sneak on them and not trusting her, because when she was younger she had not realized the things you should not say, even to your own father, because he was also the headmaster; about how she hated football and Latin, but wasn't any good at things girls were supposed to be good at either; about how no one ever wanted to partner her in anything because they were afraid of being laughed at by the other boys; and so on and so forth, in no logical order, but just as they happened to her mind; years' and years' worth, it seemed, of her miseries.

At last she said, daring to because it came in such a rush of other things and she had begun to make herself feel again so sad and tearful, 'And then I'm never good enough at things for *you* because I am a girl.'

'Good grief!' he said; then, more slowly, 'Did you think I'd rather you were a boy?'

'Wouldn't you?' she asked.

'Good grief,' he said again. He put down his pen, got up from his desk and came over to her, touched her shoulder again, but said nothing more of any consequence except, 'You'd better wash your face, Mary, before your mother sees you,' with something of a smile.

*

Later that evening when Mary was in bed, her mother

came and sat down on the bed beside her. She said nothing for a moment, just looked at Mary and sighed audibly. She did actually look very tired, thought Mary, who felt rather worn and weak herself, after so much weeping; lay nevertheless quite silently, waiting for what would come.

'You have really worried Daddy. I'm cross with you, Mary, or I ought to be. You know how busy he is at the beginning of any term – the summer term's always the worst too, the timetables are so especially complicated.' She sighed, then after a pause went on. 'I think he's making too much of it, mind; I think you have exaggerated, Mary, I do not think the matter is so serious myself. Besides, I do not believe in children making their own decisions on such matters. But he asked me to ask you ...'

'Then why didn't he ask me himself?' said Mary, picking at her sheet, the light very yellow tonight, making the sheet look yellow, reflecting little harsh and still yellower lights on it from the yellow tiles.

'Mary, what a thing to say ...'

'I'm sorry,' said Mary, and meant it a little bit.

Her mother's voice became very abrupt suddenly.

'Do you want to change schools, Mary? Go out to another school, a day school and with girls?'

Mary's mouth was literally open with astonishment. She could not believe it. 'But ...' she said.

'You do not, of course, have to make up your mind tonight. It would not in any case be possible to move you till the autumn term; and he said you were to think about it carefully, then decide for yourself. You do realize, don't you, Mary, that it would disappoint him to lose you. He values your being here at his school. As I do, Mary. I daresay you never notice. You do not seem very aware of your parents, Mary, for a great deal of the time.'

*

Next morning after breakfast her father stopped her, walking down the passage.

'I think your mother will have spoken to you, Mary. What do you think about it now?'

'I don't know. I really don't.'

'You must take your time, of course. But let me know, please, when you are ready, so that I can make definite arrangements. Or rather let your mother know.' His voice was formal and polite; he smiled his distant headmaster's smile and went away.

As for William – the evening before Mary had gone on being cross with him a little, at least had planned dramatic statements to make to him; at the thought of their actual making, felt, as she heard him walk along the passage outside her door to find her, very slightly sick, like an actor with nerves before a big performance. But William did not seem to notice any of it, hardly gave her a chance in fact to say anything at all. He was a bit like her father, she thought, *unnoticing*, and for some reason that thought made her laugh so much that she could not be properly angry any more. Though it was annoying he should be so casual, so unaware, apparently, of anything being untoward when she had, because of him, been suffering so severely.

chapter fourteen

The school next morning felt like an awakened wood when spring starts happening, even if it smelt quite different, formidably of polish. Every door was open that had been closed all through the holidays; dormitory doors through which maids could be seen scrubbing floors, washing windows, making up the beds, or one or other of the two school handymen up a ladder, whistling loudly, and fixing curtain rods and curtains; the doors of the huge cupboards along the corridors that held equally huge piles of sheets and towels and pillowcases or else stacks of lavatory paper and scouring pads and so much soap that the scent rolled out and made you dizzy as you passed. William and Mary wandered round falling over buckets and polishing cloths and mops. Chased from classroom to classroom, they ended up again finally in William's, which the tide had not as yet reached.

William stood looking at his monsters critically, then unpinned the paper and laid it down again on the teacher's table where they had worked at it yesterday, none of the desks being wide enough. Mary dug out the copy of *The Box of Delights*, which she had noticed in his desk and read it leaning on the radiator by the window. Only after a little while she found she could not concentrate, so she returned the book to its place and wandered over to see what William had done to their picture.

'Oh,' she said. 'Why have you done that?'

'Why shouldn't I?' For he had set the shell out on the paper beside a lobster with its eyes on stalks, and he had drawn beside it the shell's mirror image.

'Are you thinking we could just go into your picture and get it?' she asked. 'The other half?'

'The *other* half?'

'Yes, you've just drawn it, haven't you?'

'So I have,' he said slowly, and the implications dawning, 'Wow! So I *have*.'

'Why did you draw it like that if you didn't mean it to be the other half?'

'I don't know. How should I know?'

'But you would have to draw it among those awful creatures, wouldn't you?'

'Yes, wouldn't I. But perhaps they'll be friendly because I drew them.'

It was extraordinary how cool William was, she thought – he was actually teasing her; and then looking at him, realized he was not actually cool at all.

'I doubt it,' she said. 'If you think I'm going into that picture . . .'

'But you must.'

'No.'

'I will love you for ever, Mary.' He was glowing, dizzy-looking, the way she had never seen or imagined him.

'*No.*'

'You're a coward then . . .'

'No, I'm not.'

'I dare you.'

'I never accept dares.'

'You must accept mine. I dare you.'

'Oh, all right,' she said, caving in suddenly because she knew in the end she would have to anyway. She had been teasing too, she supposed. But she was also genuinely, actually frightened. These creatures that William had drawn were like ones you dreamed about, so woke, screaming, in the dark.

Her own whale would be better. She looked at him, at

the HOTEL WHALE across his forehead, and found him friendly-looking, even comforting. She wished William had drawn the shell beside him instead of among the crabs and the lobsters and the octopi and other less identifiable, yet horrid, things.

'It's so unbelievably simple,' William was saying in a rather awed voice. 'Just to have drawn it, for myself.'

'Well, I wish you had drawn it somewhere else, that's all.'

'So you've said. Mary, stop making such a fuss.'

'Me, a *fuss* ...' But, laughing, he had touched her hands with the shell. And it was far too late, for there they stood on a rock above a shallow dip or cave filled with creatures whose tentacles, feelers, claws, even whose eyes wavered about randomly.

'Are you actually going down among them, William?'

'I'll have to, won't I?'

'But they'll hurt you.'

'Strangled by octopus, dismembered by crab. Yes, it's a jolly prospect. Why don't you come too?'

But Mary had shut her eyes. 'I can't even bear to look at them.'

'Well, I drew them, didn't I? They're mine. And look, Mary, I can see the shell.'

'What's the good of having it, if you're dead?'

'I won't be dead. Open your eyes, Mary. That is it, isn't it?'

'I suppose so. Oh, William, it isn't worth it.'

'Come with me.'

'I couldn't.'

'I think you've got to.'

'No, William, please.' There was one huge lobster with orange feelers that looked, she thought, as if it particularly disliked her, seeming to focus its stalked and beady eyes on where she stood, waving its disproportionately huge and vicious claw as near her feet as it could. She tried to shift back, but William held her arm too tightly. 'I *can't.*'

'Come on.'

'I can't. I can't.'

'Look, you'll have to now.' For quite coolly he had held out his own shell and dropped it there among them all. Mary began to laugh a little hysterically. There was nothing else left to do. And then, as suddenly, came a wave of enormous anger. She wrenched her hand away from William, grabbed, and shook him.

'You beast, you beast. How could you, how could you? And I don't care, I'm not going down there, I'd rather spend the rest of my life here ...' And she turned and gazed away into the shadowed sea behind her and saw a huge whitish cave – only it was not a cave she realized then, it was a mouth, a huge, open and engulfing mouth.

She began to laugh again. 'My whale. I'll take my whale any day.' And she began to run across the seabed, against the water, very exhausting – it was like running against a strong wind, but for some reason it did not occur to her to swim, though the water encouraged her to, lifting and pushing her every now and then. She could feel William coming after her. And he did not swim either, though had he done so, he would have caught her easily. As it was he caught her, but just too late. For suddenly she was swimming and had swum inside the great white cave – as William grabbed her, the mouth snapped shut, they fell together on to the lower jaw, rolled over and over and over there.

They were slow to sort things out and pick themselves up. But when they did, found that inside a mouth they might be, but it was not mouthlike at all, except in shape (though they might partly have had that impression, because they were not overly familiar with the insides of mouths). It was like a great ribbed cave, arching to a point and made of some white substance set with curious spikes, which she realized in a little while were hairs; while curved around three-quarters of it or more, was a kind of indented white fence, like an uneven and widely-spaced venetian blind, only vertical. It took Mary a moment to work out what it reminded her of still more, and then she laughed because it seemed so incongruous. 'It's like an organ,' she said. 'Like organ pipes.' And then, 'Are they teeth? Pretty funny-looking teeth.'

There were cushioned sofas all round the walls, and a large somewhat undulating and fleshy carpet down the middle from front to back, which again Mary, having stared uncomprehendingly, realized must be its tongue. 'Does that make us its *food*?' she thought, with a kind of distant alarm, but as much amusement. Then William took her arm and led her across to a large but empty desk that, like everything else, was curved to the shape of the ribbed and corrugated walls. It was labelled 'Reception', and decorated with sprays of seaweed in a small shell vase. Propped against that stood a notice, which said in large and curly letters, HOTEL WHALE. And in smaller letters underneath, 'For service please ring bell. Then proceed through bead curtain and down passage to inner hall where we shall be happy to meet your requirements. SERVICE IS OUR MOTTO.' There was an arrow too, pointing to the rear, where indeed hung a bead curtain, made out of what looked like dull yellow stones, each strand swaying a little, hiding a long rounded passage, dimly lit, that led into the whale's interior.

'Well,' said William. 'There doesn't seem any other way out, does there, Mary?' So, both rather reluctant but quite resigned, they walked through the bead curtain, down the passage whose light had no obvious source, glowing from the walls themselves as if they were luminous.

The inner hall was much like the outer, except that its walls were smoother and it lacked the organ pipes. But they hardly had time to take it in, because as soon as they arrived, they were assaulted by a sound so vast, so very strange, it took them some time to realize that the succession of sounds made speech, that they were indeed inside a voice – a very curious and uncomfortable sensation, for the sounds emerged from every part of every surface round them, like multiple stereophony.

'It's coming out of my skin,' said Mary, her hands over her ears, which did not help to deaden it at all, so much more than her ears being assaulted.

But the sounds resolved themselves into words at last, saying quite clearly, 'Do you require rooms for the night?'

Mary would have replied no, automatically. But William, grinning broadly, said, 'Yes, *please*.'

'But we don't . . .'

'Well, you shut us in here, didn't you? And we've got to sit here in a whale's belly. We might as well be comfortable.'

'It's like being eaten.'

'And whose fault is that?' William was saying, when the voice broke out, spoke through them again, or so it seemed.

'Eaten?' it said indignantly. 'Whatever do you mean *eaten*? I am not quite a vegetarian. But I eat no meat of your kind or size, having none of your barbaric weapons which you call teeth.'

'Then what are those things in your mouth?' asked Mary.

'Ah, that is a very neat, very satisfactory arrangement,' said the whale. 'That is a means of filtering my food, so I take in only what is wholesome and appropriate, the smallest, most innocuous of animals. But that need not concern you in any case. What I have to offer you is board and lodgings. The bedrooms, I assure you, are clean and comfortable, with all conveniences and running water, naturally.'

And so they were, pink and white rooms, the outside walls slightly curved again and ribbed, the beds fitted in against them like bunks. 'Well, I suppose they would be,' William said, 'whales and ships being shaped somewhat the same.' The running water also, delightfully, did not so much run as spout up from the centre of basins made out of what looked like huge oyster shells when you pressed on brass handles, very highly polished. 'Just like the whale's spout,' said Mary.

'You must admit,' she said, 'my drawing's ended up much more comfortable than yours. If Jonah's whale was like this, he must have enjoyed himself.'

'Are you enjoying yourself?' asked William, examining a long list headed House Rules, pinned up on a cupboard door.

'Sort of. It's quite nice here.' Mary came over to read the list of rules too. It began with an obvious one, considering where they were: 'Kindly do not jump or bounce' and ended: 'To gain admittance after midnight, please ask for key to door by 7th filter bone along.' But meanwhile William had moved on to look at some of the prints hung around the walls, framed in small and varnished seashells, most of them, astonishingly, showing a single subject. Mary, following him to see, could not believe her eyes at first. 'Whaling,' she said. 'Whaling, of *all* things.' But in each case the whale seemed distinctly to come off best. In one, a boat full of men was contained within the very jaws of a whale. In another, the boat was tilted by the lashing of a huge tail, the fishermen falling headlong into the water. 'More like *menning*,' said William with satisfaction. 'And so it should be. There are far more men about actually than whales.'

'Hadn't you better look at all the shells, in case?'

'What, with mine out there? Oh, all right,' William said, and shrugged. On every surface, she'd noticed, were set out shells – as ashtrays or for hairpins, she supposed.

'You look here. I'll try the other room,' he said. Music began to play as Mary searched, coming from some hidden loudspeaker – selections from *South Pacific*, followed by the 'Sailors' Hornpipe', making her hum gently to herself. And none of the shells resembled William's in the slightest. As she finished examining the last, William appeared but shook his head at her when she looked at him inquiringly.

'Now what?' he asked. Mary knew it was inevitable, always had known, sighed a little as she looked at the soft light and the comfort round her.

'I suppose we have to go and pick up yours again,' she said.

'I thought you'd rather stay here all your life.'

'In a way. But . . .'

'Then how do you suggest we get out of here?'

'Well, if you can get in again after midnight, presumably you can get out now. Why don't we press the button for the manager and ask?'

'Are you still scared?'

'Well, what do you think? Yes, of course, I am.'

'What you drew turned out all right; perhaps my monsters won't be so bad when it comes to it. Perhaps they won't be like real lobsters and crabs and things. After all, this is not exactly like a real whale.'

'Shall I press the button for the manager? It says you can.'

'What do we want him for?'

'To ask our way out, silly,' said Mary, pressing the red button under the list of rules. At which the huge, yet when you got used to it, rather gentle and soothing voice assailed them again. 'And what can I do to accommodate you now?' it said.

And so there they were again, facing William's monsters. And again as the claws and tentacles waved about and waved, Mary shuddered and shivered and said, 'No, I *can't.*' And, 'Suppose the shell isn't there any more,' she said. 'Suppose it's gone, eaten, anything; suppose we get in there for nothing? Oh, William, why did you have to be so *stupid.*' Amid her fear the anger rose in her again; so did the still greater fear that both their shells would have gone. Yet she did not care any longer about the one he'd drawn, only the one that represented their route back into the real world. William smiled at her now, took his hand away from her, and, with a little nonchalant wave, jumped down right on top of the largest lobster of all. And she, so angry and frightened together that she hardly cared any more, certainly did not think any more, she took off, giving a great yell, and jumped down there too – and did not immediately feel nipped or pinched or bitten or snaked about by tentacles, indeed just met an unpleasant grind and crunch and then nothing whatever at all, except the sound of more grindings and crunchings and splittings and tearings, the most unexpected sounds in the circumstances. And so she opened her eyes again, not expecting, not knowing what she might see or why.

'I told you they wouldn't be real,' said William, as she opened them. And he was waving a lobster's claw right under her nose, and as she looked, he clasped it with the other hand and pulled it apart so easily it might have been paper, indeed it was paper, or rather a very thick cardboard. At the same time he was kicking with his feet. 'Kick,' he said. 'If you don't want to pick things up, just kick.'

She looked down first. Beneath her feet was a sad mess of what looked like papier mâché and waste paper – and she saw other bits, of lobster, crab, or octopus, flying everywhere, only they were not the flesh or the armour of real creatures; they were painted paper and cardboard and plaster and clay, and so kick, kick, kick, she began also, and snap, crack, snap, more of them broke, flew apart at the touch of her feet. It was like a dream. It was not real at all, as William said.

'How could they be real when I invented them?' William bent down and picked up his own shell. At the same time, half-hidden beneath a severed but still unpleasantly convincing claw, Mary saw the other and forgot her fear in the excitement and picked it up. But it was already pulpy and limp and fell apart between her fingers, for it was paper like all the rest, and she held out the fragments to William, wordlessly.

'Still, it was a nice idea,' he said. 'Fortunately, my shell is real still,' and he had them back in the classroom instantly, where all that was left of their frieze was torn bits of paper, mostly littering the floor, except for one piece, the one containing Mary's whale, which hung askew on the board on a single drawing pin.

'My whale wasn't paper,' she said. 'It couldn't have been. Why wasn't it?'

'But it wasn't real, any more than my monsters were; you couldn't have a hotel inside a whale; you just drew a different sort of unrealness, that's all. I suppose there would be different sorts of unrealness.'

'And different sorts of realness, I suppose too,' said Mary thoughtfully, who had never thought of such a thing before and was not altogether sure now whether she liked it.

chapter fifteen

Nearer and nearer all the time, and yet still as far as ever, for they only had the half of William's shell. Had she been William, Mary thought, she would have been very upset at what had happened that morning – she found she minded herself, rather, despite still not knowing why they had to find it. It had seemed such a simple, such an obvious solution, the kind where everything appears to fall neatly into place, and you wonder why you have never thought of such a thing before – only you haven't, not at all. And so, for the second time, the shell appeared to have been within William's grasp. And then not: the hope had crumbled literally to nothing.

But if William was upset, as usual he did not show it. Indeed, he was apparently at his most careless and cheerful, and he would not discuss the shell at all, though they had only one more day to find it in. And she found this irritating because she wanted to discuss it, as well as being puzzled by his cheerfulness.

'Do you think we should go and say goodbye to people?' he had said after lunch.

'*Goodbye?* Whoever to?'

'Mr Penney. Miss Pitt. Mrs Trent.'

'But we see Miss Pitt and Mr Penney every day in termtime – while we're here, of course,' she added, thinking she might not be next term.

'But it's not the same in termtime, is it quite?'

'Isn't it? Anyway Mr Penney won't let us into the kitchen now, not now they're all so busy.'

'Let's try Miss Pitt first.' But Miss Pitt was not there –

her door open, the room empty; something Mary hardly regretted, since she could not really see what William meant about the need to say goodbye, having just sat next to Miss Pitt at lunch and being likely to sit next to or opposite her at supper tonight and breakfast and lunch tomorrow. Mr Penney, however, whom they sought out next, was standing at the door of his kitchen with his back to them, surveying the actions of his kitchen staff within, much as a producer might watch his actors on a stage; and maintaining his own silence in the middle of all their talk and clatter, shifting from one tennis-shoed foot to the other, soundlessly; then suddenly letting out the most enormous bellow, which drowned the rest and was the more effective and startling for coming from such silence. The whole kitchen fell still, momentarily. But the performance continued with a slight shift and alteration somewhere, as if the workers had responded like actors, tackling the same tasks just a little differently, though how, whether they cleaned ovens or saucepans with different kinds of strokes or what, it was hard to say exactly.

William went boldly and touched him on the shoulder. He spun round. Mary expected him to say go away, not with words necessarily, just actions, but he said only, 'What can I do for you then, my lads?'

'We've come to say goodbye.'

'He thinks we need to because it's termtime tomorrow,' said Mary to protect William, a desire she had had in there before, which was odd because she did not consider William someone who needed protecting. But she did not want Mr Penney now to think him absolutely mad.

'It's not the same in termtime,' William said. Mr Penney looked at him for a long moment, then turned away to survey his world, and spoke to them at last but over his shoulder.

'Maybe you have something there, lad. You mean like

we are two selves, one put away in term, the other in the holidays, our lives not being the same? It's true – I feel pretty much different when I've my kitchen to myself – not that some corners of it aren't mine and no one else's. But what you feel then, that's your business: how should I know that? Just you wait a bit,' he said. And he went away and came back out of that place full of machines and implements for feeding giants – or so they appeared – with a small battered tin of human size, a picture of Windsor Castle on its lid, and took from it two Maryland cookies, one for each of them.

So they went off then, eating them, to find Mrs Trent, whom Mary, as ever, had no desire to see at all, only she could feel it was rightful so gave no objections. They went to the Café first but found only the boy, who offered to sell them crisps at a penny off since he still had none of the cheese and onion flavour, and then guessed Mrs Trent was upstairs in her tower, though he wasn't too certain. So they climbed the ladderlike stairs up to her front door and banged on it loudly. There was silence for a long time. Mary had a sudden hope Mrs Trent might not be in either, but as William lifted his hand to the knocker for the second time, the door fell open and left him empty-handed with his arm still raised, while she loomed in the doorway like someone in the mirrors on the pier, so odd-looking she did not need distorting mirrors, thought Mary savagely, and was ashamed of thinking that, even as she realized why she had, Mrs Trent today having a mouth lined with pins that looked as if she was growing bigger teeth from seed.

'Oh, it's you, dearies, do come in,' she said indistinctly, though removing some. 'I was just upstairs pinning Mrs Taylor's new costume on her dummy, that's what made me take so long, getting down the stairs and my old legs. I'll finish it now, if you wouldn't mind, but you're welcome to keep me company as I do, my ducks.'

So they climbed the second set of ladder stairs and came out into the light of the sky and leaned on the windows, watching her and sea alternately. More pins than ever were bristling from her mouth. Mary wondered how she could talk without swallowing any, was alarmed in case, yet curious to know what would happen if she did. Mrs Trent must have been out quite recently, for she still wore her beret on her head but had changed into slippers at the other end with rather grubby pink fur round their edges and crinkled rubber soles, revealed when she kneeled on the floor to pin Mrs Taylor's hem. After a while she clambered to her feet and made Mary come and hold more pins for her, standing level to the dummy's shoulder; a very stout lady, Mrs Taylor, prominently bosomed, her form now swathed in a dark green wool with a bright pink bobble in it. Outside, behind Mary, screamed the gulls. She heard the sea's faint wash too and, turning, saw the sea and gulls.

'That's it then,' said Mrs Trent at last, patting the dummy and lifting off the green cloth. 'And now, how would you feel, my doves, about a cup of tea?'

William sat down with them at the table this time. But he had taken a shell first, from the mantelpiece, one of the shiny freckled ones, and he turned it over and over in his hands.

'Find your own shell, did you then?'

'No,' he said. 'We didn't.'

'Did you expect it, do you still? Is it your lucky time, did you think?'

William shook his head. 'I don't know, I really don't.'

'Ah well, that's sensible enough, my duck. Don't you bother either way, I'd say. Have a biscuit. I thought you might be in, I got some chocolate. Here and now is better than any heart's desire, though I don't doubt you have one and hope you achieve it soon, with shells or not,' she said, looking at William who turned scarlet to Mary's astonishment and choked upon a crumb. But she had no time to reflect on it, because Mrs Trent had turned to her and said, 'And you, ducky, have you one, or are you easy about things?' And to her equal astonishment, she found she couldn't think of any, not now, sitting here with William, eating chocolate biscuits. Certainly if she had a heart's desire, it was nothing to do with schools or changing schools, she realized, which was the only thing she could think of immediately, the problem being somewhat on her mind. For she still did not know what she was going to tell her father. She said, 'I don't know, I don't,' and shook her head both to that and Mrs Trent.

'You can keep that shell, William love, as a souvenir of our good time on the pier; worse than Dracula we looked, and no luck either on the machines, but it was enjoyable. And you too, Mary dovie, choose one for yourself.'

But as Mary was examining the shells, wondering if she might take two if she chose little ones, she heard William ask, 'Why do you live here, Mrs Trent, right on top of the sea? Do you like the sea?' He had asked Mr Penney the same question, and Mr Penney had said rather crossly, 'Whatever do you think, my lad?' And then, more mildly, 'I'm used to it. It's independent, goes its own way, no matter how we organize the land. I care for that.' But Mrs Trent said, 'I was offered it, dovie, wasn't I, this roof over my head. Yes' (or 'Yace').

'And you really like it?'

'I'm used to it, but I wouldn't say I don't fancy a nice bungalow sometimes, those steps down here don't do my old legs much good, or trade if it comes to that, if I've work enough to occupy.'

*

When they left Mrs Trent, it felt, Mary thought, as if her

room came with them for a little while. Its heavy musty smell seemed to hang about them. Every now and then she caught a whiff of it.

'Now for Miss Pitt,' said William, determinedly.

'But why? She's just Miss Pitt, and we'll see her at suppertime. I don't see why we have to go and see her now.'

'But I want to. I feel like it.'

'But *why*?'

'Why not?'

'She looks so *ridiculous*.'

'She can't help that.'

'I know. But she can be really very silly. She irritates my parents, I can see it sometimes. And I've seen you laughing at her too.'

'I think she's a bit sad. I think she's lonely.'

'Miss Pitt *lonely*? But she lives with us.'

'You wouldn't notice, Mary. I observe you never notice things like that.'

'And I suppose you mean you do. Anyway, she's got her niece in Australia.'

'Does your uncle in Borneo stop you being lonely, Mary?'

'I haven't got an uncle in Borneo.'

'That's what I mean. What difference would it make if you did have one?'

'I don't know what you're talking about, William.'

'Hurray, hurray, hurray,' said William and led her on anyway to see Miss Pitt, who sat, it suddenly occurred to Mary, in a room quite full of things that spoke, and not just the typewriter: a clock with a slightly uneven tick, a small electric fire, and just now another sound, which turned out to be a plastic carrier full of chemists' goods that fell over, very slowly as she sat by it. William did not sit down at once but leaned on a filing cabinet bearing a china cat, a pottery bowl full of paper clips and drawing pins, a pottery jug filled with an enormous quantity of sharpened pencils, and a small photograph in a large gilt frame – 'My niece in Australia,' said Miss Pitt, as William looked at it – and he glanced across at Mary and very briefly grinned.

She had been flustered but delighted to see them again, looking up in surprise from a heap of paper. When William had explained his mission, she gestured so widely and bewilderedly she succeeded in knocking the whole lot on the floor, and they all banged heads in picking them up again.

'But I'll see you every day of term,' she said. And, 'Wait, I think I've got some peppermints,' which she had, the curiously strong, digestive kind that Mary hated, but after William's lecture did not feel she should refuse. The whole room was filled with the scent of peppermint. Why did grown-ups always think they had to offer you food as a greeting, Mary thought, though it was all right when you liked the food, certainly.

'Come and look at the magazines when you like, William and Mary. No need to knock.'

'Let's look at them now,' said William unexpectedly. 'It isn't supper yet. May we look at them?'

And so they did, not searching now for anything in particular. But lying on the floor companionably, they pointed out to each other such unlikely things as four-eyed fish, or Africans who liked their women quite grotesquely fat; Miss Pitt from time to time interrupting her typing to come and see what they had found. Even the dust did not seem so unpleasant. Sneezing was interesting, Mary decided, who had never thought much about a sneeze before. She felt quite extraordinarily contented and contained. If she had a heart's desire, it must be this, she thought, to lie like this with William, companioned, what could possibly be better? Altogether it had been a good five days, almost the best five days of her whole life, and not simply because of the magic either. But she did not like to think about tomorrow. She simply would not think about tomorrow or about changing schools or anything like that; and William, anyway, was showing them now a deep-sea diving machine. They became very giggly eventually, all three of them, and went into supper like a party.

chapter sixteen

Next morning William was how she had expected him to be the day before, very silent, a little hunched and wretched-looking, keeping his hands in his pockets. 'Walk?' he had asked Mary after breakfast. They had fetched anoraks and gone down the alleyways towards the sea without either of them saying very much. Mary carried the bustle of termtime in her head – at three o'clock that day, the arrivals would begin. Against that now she set the sea and beach and William.

They walked further this time than they had walked

before, to where the shingle stopped at a breakwater. Beyond was low and slippery rock and some sand exposed by the low tide, smooth and firm and shiny in places, reflecting sky. The breakwaters beyond were made of rusty metal instead of stone. There was a jumble of concrete blocks, tipped at angles. They looked like groups of little pyramids and threw upon each other pyramid-shaped shadows. The ones nearest the sea, continually taken by the tide and exposed again were dark green with algae, those behind bleached white by wind and salt.

At the back of the beach the white cliff face had names and dates carved along it, and at the top was a length of an unusually smooth wall made of red brick and following the shape of the slope not with curves but with shallow angles, in one of which was set a small square turret.

'It looks like the great wall of China,' William said, as they scrambled up to sit there, looking out to sea. 'Whatever do you think it's for?'

'My father said they meant to make some kind of garden, only the war came and they never finished it. So there's just the wall.' Mary pointed out to sea. 'Look at all those gulls,' she said – for from up here they could see beyond the rusty breakwaters, round the edge of a cliff to where a patch of sea was thick with them, screaming and quarrelling; their wings broke out here and there from the mass of bodies, flapping wildly, sometimes actually lifting them off the surface of the sea where they would hover, feet dangling, until they found another space and settled down again among the others.

'I suppose there's a lot of fish,' said Mary.

'Sewage,' said William, 'where the sewage comes out.'

'Oh, how horrid.'

'Why? It's natural. To us and gulls. I mean gulls liking it. Shall we go down to the beach now, Mary?'

They sat in silence on the concrete blocks. It was a

grey, dull day. Rain came flirting in the wind, and went. They sat motionless, merely huddling on their hoods through a brief rainstorm, which swept along the coastline, through and past them, and vanished in the distance, the only time they could not see its limits and its brevity was when they were actually inside it. The rain hung from them in drops. The sun glanced out, made the drops glitter, disappeared. They were grey and dull again, like the beach and like the sea. Beyond their breakwater the shingle was dark and damp from the rain, the sea mild, waveless, shineless. The first day of the summer term, thought Mary; perhaps her last term; cricket and swimming and tea in the garden for a treat. But it did not feel like that at all.

'So what are we going to do?' William was saying at last. 'It's absolutely our last chance.'

'Did you think of anything at all?'

'Did you?'

'Well, no.'

'Well, neither did I.'

'Think,' said Mary. 'Think. Think.' But immediately she said, 'Don't. I do know already.' And she did, with absolute certainty, all at once, from nothing. 'Do you remember? In the aquarium. We said we hadn't been in the real sea?' and she was pointing out there, into the horizon.

'Into this real sea? Sewage and all?'

'We can walk back the other way a bit.' She got up and pulled William with her. She was shivering, heavy in her stomach and a little sick suddenly from apprehension. But she knew it had to be. And they clambered back over the breakwater and walked along the shingle and then down towards the tide.

'I must be psychic,' said William. 'My torch fell out of my drawer this morning, and I brought it. It will be very dark.'

'Hold the shell. Let me hold it with you, too.'

They walked down the beach and into the sea. The real sea. Deep, deep into it. The waters closing over their heads. But they could breathe easily, they did not even feel wet. They walked, then as weed thickened, rose above it, swam – only it was more as if they were carried along, they found themselves going at such speed over deep foliage and rock. They saw huge shadows in the distance – they did not know of what, did not want to know, but the sinister shadows never came too close. They crossed whole underwater landscapes, great forests of weed and ranges of mountains, some so big they saw only their roots, the summits reaching out above the surface of the sea. They saw deep valleys and shallow ones, great gullies and ravines, and then came out above an endless plain, stretching into dark as far as they could see.

And as their bodies could move so easily through this world, so their eyes too took on supernormal powers. They were like cats or owls, able to use the most infinitesimal amounts of light to help them see what lay about. For the water grew ever darker, the further they went on. From green it became quite colourless, heavy as a twilight turning into night, then a deeper and deeper blue, then at last it was wholly black. But in each zone of colour there were overlapping worlds where quite different kinds of creatures lived and died. The deeper they went, the more extraordinary the worlds became, like countries you imagined way beyond the stars. They'd seen fish at first that they recognized, iridescent like the water, silver and blue and green, but as the colour left the water, so it left the fish: they too were grey and lightless like the sea. And then – they were in the deep twilight now, which made it all the more startling – suddenly all around were fish like miniature airliners, for they had rows of lights along them like portholes; you almost expected to see people peering out. Often you could not see the bodies of the fish at all, only their little lines of lights, and there were other lines of light defining other weirder and more alarming shapes, creatures with feelers or tentacles or claws.

Deeper still, midnight-blue water now; and Mary saw a lobster, at least, though very small, she thought it was a lobster, it had a lobster's tail and claws; but at the same time it glowed, it was lit like a lamp from within itself and was all transparent as if made of glass. And there were others; the sea seemed full of such glassy creatures, jelly-fish and worms and squid, as well as the lobsters and some creatures like prawns besides, each one self-lit, each one having all its organs displayed inside, and each a miniature, at the most inches long. To see them as well as she was able to, Mary thought her eyes must have developed magnifying powers besides.

But she was not altogether sure she liked seeing as clearly as she did. So much strangeness at once was not comfortable. She wished she could look at William for a change, but since he had no internal lights he was almost invisible; she strained her eyes towards him desperately, in vain.

Deeper and deeper they went; into darkness so thick it seemed to come from inside their own heads: stone silence, bitter cold. Once she felt a wave of such total fear, she would at that moment have turned and fled – but holding William's hand was able to steady herself, just. Alone it would have been quite unbearable, but she was not alone, not quite.

For no strength came from William. Or none that she could feel. There was only her own strength and not so very much of that, just a certainty that was so hard and awkward, almost nubbly, it was touchable, like something right outside herself; and which said, you must go on, you must not stop. So having for a moment closed her eyes against the dark, she opened them again and continued, leading William. He did not hold back exactly, but it felt like leading him. For he was not willing, not at all.

And now the darkness was filled with tiny moving lights; gay-coloured but not gay, sinister rather, since you did not know what was making them; purple and orange and blue and silver lights, single ones or grouped, some quite brilliant, others dim, while others were broader, fuzzier, like a glow across the dark. She grabbed William's torch from him again and swung it round: it picked up still more startling and unlikely colours, purple and orange and scarlet. There were scarlet shrimps six inches long at least, and a crimson squid, there were violet-striped jelly-fish and purple things like bolsters with fringes underneath. And there were eyes, like head-lamps some of them, huge and faceted, staring blindly at the night.

The eyes were bad enough; but it was not the eyes that were so important here or the brilliant colours even. It was the mouths. This world was all of gaping mouths, mouths like caves and as big as the bodies that wore them, viciously bristling, fanged like dragons; mouths swallowing other mouths, no smaller than themselves, black bellies distended to accommodate such prey. Even the lights seemed made to serve the mouths, for they dangled on lines enticingly, luring other fishes in.

They did not threaten Mary, all these mouths and teeth. They belonged to fish only inches long that no matter how hungry or how savage could not have encompassed live human dinners. Yet she did not find that comforting; she did not like those mouths and teeth; she did not like to contemplate such savagery; it made a world too cruel for her to bear. And she and William were the only monsters in it.

And then that too was altogether gone. There was

nothing except them and the dark and cold. William's hand, which had been gripping Mary's more and more tightly, now dragged altogether, hardly let her move. And his voice reached her out of the darkness, with terrifying echoes and distortions in it.

'I can't. I can't. I must go back.'

'We must go on.' She tugged at his hand, but still he hung there in the darkness, he would not come. And suddenly she realized he was not going to unless she made him. He had given up. There was only her.

She could not endure it. For a moment she almost gave in to him, turned back the other way. She was surprised to find herself saying, '*Yes*, William,' and tugging at him still. Then she stuffed the torch back in his pocket and gripped his hand with both of hers. It was the only proof she could give him that she was real; her voice simply sounded ghostly, as did his. But his hands were still recognizable flesh and blood to her. If that was so, then hers must be so to him.

The sea was a great weight in and around them. It could have been rock, it was no less solid. Yet they had to go on through it, down and down.

'Mary, I *can't*.' The pure childish terror in William's voice reached her, distorted as it was, frightening her more than anything had done. Yet, curiously, that also gave her strength, because if she gave way, too, then they would be wholly lost. She tugged at him again, willing him to come, and this time, having resisted her once more, he obeyed at last and suddenly came on.

And they were there at last. They stood far down on the deep seabed; as far from men in mind and journeying as the moon itself.

'Your torch, William.' But he stood there trembling, motionless, so again she fumbled in his pocket and took from him the torch and shone it out, such a feeble, silly little light, as if in the whole sky there was only a single star and that a billion billion miles away. It picked out a space around their feet, a space empty of monsters, of anything even particularly strange. They saw pebbles like those on their own beach, sand, mud, ordinary, unexceptional. Something moved a little way away, and this startled them at first but only momentarily, for it turned out to be a flatfish like the ones in the aquarium, caught just off their coasts; greyish and mottled, like the seabed, and similar to a sole or dab or plaice, its gills moving gently, up and down.

There were shells too. But not William's. She realized she had not expected to find it here. That was not why they had had to come. William was still quivering wretchedly beside her, and so she put her arms round him and hugged him hard. She had never done that in her life – put her arms round someone, hugged them, just like that. Even here she felt ridiculous. But it did not stop her, she did not take her arms away; for stupid or not, she knew it was necessary. And still he stood shaking, just a little, his arms straight down beside him; then for a moment put them up and hugged her back, and it was so quick she did not know afterwards whether she had dreamed it. But she let him go anyway, flicked off the torch, which had beamed on the seabed crooked all the while, found his anorak pocket, stuffed it back. And suddenly, she had bent to the seabed where the beam had fallen, stretched out her hand and, finding something, picked it up, and put it secretly in the pocket of her own anorak.

And now once more she took William's hand. And led him in darkness back the way they had come; past the regions of the midget monsters, the lanternlike glassy ones, the mini-airliners; through the plains and valleys, beside the roots of mountains and the summits of mountains, the weed jungles, the huge but distant forms, the shoals of fish, the terrors they could see and the terrors they could not.

Back into seeing with ordinary eyes; Mary realized it long after she had begun to see. It happened so slowly, the light so dim and grey at first it was hardly light, its colours all sucked out; then gradually there was silver, green, and blue and white.

Overhead they remembered, at last, there stood the sun.

They walked out of the sea, quite dry, both of them, up the beach towards the red wall, stumbling on the stones and blinking. But as they passed a little patch of sand, William said suddenly, 'Stop, idiot, look, *look*.' And he bent down and pulled it out, a shell nearly bedded, but not too far, for it was his shell, the other half of it. He fitted them together then and there – it was like a torn page mended, each crack and indentation matched and fitted.

They stood and looked at one another. Then, abruptly, William sat down and Mary followed, the pebbles shifting under her and feeling slightly damp. She watched William take the shells apart and fit them together, apart and together, over and over again. After a while he stopped and handed them to her and she did it too, marvelling at the exactness and obviousness of it, pretty soon hardly able to imagine what it had been like without both of them together: especially as nothing else had changed meanwhile. The sea moved placidly in front of them; behind the sea-wall the unseen town awaited their return.

But she was worried about William at first. He still looked dreadfully white, she thought he might be ill.

'How extraordinarily stupid of us, Mary, not to have looked for it on our own beach,' he said. 'It would have saved us an awful lot of trouble.' He got to his feet – and suddenly she saw there was no need to worry any more, for even as she watched his face was turning pink and his eyes brightening. 'Thank you Mary,' he said quietly. And he actually began to run up the beach over the dragging stones, Mary panting unhappily after him; tore up the alleys, growing ever pinker and pinker in the face and ever more dishevelled. He did not stop until he reached the front step. Then he smoothed his hair down, seemed even to cool the brightness of his eyes, pointed at a car standing by the kerb, saying, 'I knew they'd come if I found it,' walked up the steps and in at the front door, very slowly and deliberately, and said coolly to the couple standing in the hall, 'And when did you two happen to arrive?'

*

Mary left them to it – William and his parents. She went on up the stairs alone, resigned. Had the shell brought them? Were they coming in any case? It really did not matter, she decided. To have done all they had, to have found the shell, that was important in itself.

What had she wanted from it for herself, she wondered. But though she still did not know, there was one small thing decided for her now, and she proposed to deal with that immediately. She looked down over the banisters at William's mother and father, who were talking to him like dear friends at a party, only noisier, and thought what was the point of going to the school with girls. They would not necessarily be more companionable; she was just as likely to find herself alone. She was used to being solitary, she was solitary anyway, she'd stay here, why ever not? Beyond that she didn't know a thing.

She did not propose to tell her mother, either. She meant to announce it to her father, to his face. She went straight to his study door and banged on it. Seeing her, he said quite amiably, 'Can you wait a moment, Mary? I won't be long, I promise you.'

And so, while waiting outside his door, she remembered it at last and put her hand into her anorak pocket and found what she had gathered and drew it out – a perfect five-pointed, brittle star, smaller than her palm and rough to her fingers most pleasingly. And when she licked it, it tasted salt.

Penelope Lively

The Ghost of Thomas Kempe 35p

Thomas Kempe was a seventeenth-century sorcerer who returns in the form of a poltergeist when the Harrison family move to an old cottage. James, their ten-year-old son, is blamed for all the tricks this meddlesome ghost gets up to, but it is not until he uncovers the reason for Thomas Kempe's reappearance that he finds a way to lay the ghost for ever.

Winner of the 1973 Library Association Carnegie Medal for an outstanding book for children.

Astercote 35p

The Cotswold village of Astercote was wiped out in the fourteenth century by the Black Death – and its ruins now lie hidden in the murky wood. But when Peter and Mair Jenkins discover it, and its secret 'Thing', they find themselves caught up in an atmosphere of medieval superstition that becomes a frightening reality.

The Whispering Knights 35p

When Martha, William and Susie concoct a magic brew, they unwittingly invoke the enmity of Morgan le Fay, the notorious enchantress who is posing as the wife of a local tycoon. She uses all her powers of evil against them, and only the Whispering Knights and the mysterious Miss Hepplewhite can save them from a terrible fate.

Penelope Lively

The Driftway 40p

When Paul runs away from home, he travels along the Driftway, an ancient route between Banbury and Northampton. He soon discovers that this road has messages for those who can hear them. The words he hears and the people he encounters have a very special meaning for him.

The Wild Hunt of Hagworthy 40p

Lucy goes to stay with her aunt in a village where they are reviving the ancient 'Horn Dance' to raise money for the Church. The revival begins as a kind of joke but as the days get hotter and hotter Lucy realizes that there is an underlying sinister tone and that she must do something about it before it is too late. Rumour has it that the Wild Hunt has been heard again – ghost hounds and antlered horsemen – brought back by the revival of the Horn Dance.

Monica Dickens

The House at World's End 35p

Rather than stay with relations in a grey London suburb, the Fielding children – Tom, Carrie, Em and Michael – decide to live by themselves in a tumbledown country pub. There are thrilling moments and frightening ones, too, as the house at World's End becomes a haven for sick, stray or ill-treated animals.

Spring Comes to World's End 35p

As their Uncle Rudolph threatens to deprive them of their beloved World's End, the Fielding children try to earn the money to buy it themselves. But money disappears as fast as it comes in, and it is not until the children are at the point of despair that their home is saved in a dramatic and exciting climax.

Monica Dickens

World's End in Winter 35p

More adventures of the Fielding children, with their family of animals. Their first winter at World's End is packed with incident and excitement that involves children and animals alike.

Summer at World's End 35p

The Fielding children are still on their own, still caring for any animal in distress. Lack of money is a problem while some unwanted visitors add to the fun – and the excitement.

Follyfoot 40p

Life can never be dull for young Callie or her family. There is always so much to do on the farm – tending unwanted horses, providing mounts for film companies, schooling ponies, helping unlucky holidaymakers, and keeping a wary eye on the unscrupulous owners of the Pinecrest riding stables.

Dora at Follyfoot 40p

'Don't buy any horses' – it was easy for the Captain to lay down rules before he went away to convalesce leaving Dora and Steve in charge. But rules are made to be broken and Dora knows she must buy Amigo, the rangy scarred cream-coloured horse, even if it means borrowing money from Ron Stryker. To pay Ron back, someone from Follyfoot just has to win the Moonlight Pony Steeplechase.

Honor Arundel

The High House 40p

When her mother and father are killed in a car crash thirteen-year-old Emma goes to live with her aunt in Edinburgh. Aunt Patsy is a freelance designer and is always waiting for the next cheque to arrive. To begin with Emma finds it difficult to adjust to the new way of life – but soon she begins to enjoy it.

Emma's Island 40p

Emma is now living on the island of Stranday, and has problems. Then the summer brings Alastair, a student from Glasgow, and Emma falls in love for the very first time.

Emma in Love 40p

Back in Edinburgh again, Emma is now keeping house for her student brother and studying hard at school, as well as continuing her exciting friendship with Alastair.